HIGH HEEL LEADERSHIP

THE ART OF BEING A WOMAN IN POWER

NATASHA S. HAMPTON

Disclaimer:

The advice found within may not be suitable for every individual. This work is purchased with the understanding that neither the author nor the publisher, are held responsible for any results. Neither author nor publisher assumes responsibility for errors, omissions or contrary interpretations of the subject matter herein. Any perceived disparagement of an individual or organization is misinterpretation.

Brand and product names mentioned are trademarks that belong solely to their respective owners.

Photo credits:

Back of book photo by: Jharder Photography
Head shot by: Ronald L. Sowers Photography

Library of Congress Cataloging-in-Publication Data under ISBN: Below are the book ISBNs.

Paperback: ISBN: 978-1-7341214-2-1
Hardcover: ISBN: 978-1-7341214-3-8
Digital: ISBN: 978-1-7341214-5-2

Table of Contents

FOREWORD

I got to know Ms. Hampton during the International City Governance Conference in Qingdao of China in 2019. We were two 'high heels' participating in the summit dialogue on big data and city governance. I, as the host, was deeply impressed by her insightful understanding and arguments on this issue. More importantly, her proposition of awareness promoting women's leadership cast a new light on understanding big data and city governance. Her stance and powerful delivery resonated with applause from conference attendees, both men and women. From our first meeting, Natasha fueled my passion and interest to explore women's leadership in China. Her newly released book arrived at exactly the time to answer my questions like, how to prepare to be a woman in leadership, how to develop our abilities and how to fully and confidently self-promote on our road to power. Her book depicts and presents the landscape and solutions for all women who share the same vision of being a woman in leadership, and bridges vision and action brilliantly. Maybe it is time we prepare to be women leaders rather than over-focus on the limitations. The time is now to recognize and be empowered by our abilities, rather than stalled by worries.

Dongfang (Linda) Wang

Ph.D.

Executive Director of ICMA China Center

Associate Professor, China University of Political Science and Law

INTRODUCTION

This book is written to paint a more candid picture of women on the leadership landscape. It will discuss ways that women can be effective, well-rounded, leaders. This is a bird's-eye view of the topic to provide those in supporting, and lead, roles a solid blueprint for their individual advancement.

Many women have struggled to acquire a seat at the boardroom table. The road to a position of power has weakened the strongest of women. Still, they fight, no matter the limitations, for every opportunity. Most often they encounter something, or someone, that appears ready to block their path.

What if I told you that your seat has always been available? You don't need permission to sit down, but you've been waiting for it. This seat requires no invitation. Stop waiting for one. You can have that seat, right now. Are you ready to take it?

I beat the odds and achieved what data suggested I could not, or would find challenging to overcome. I was a teen mom, welfare recipient, first semester college dropout and ultimately homeless. According to the National Conference of State Legislatures, teenage mothers are likely to live in poverty, depend on public assistance and their children are more likely to have lower school achievement, enter the child welfare and correctional systems, drop out of high school and become teen parents themselves.[1]

I literally started from the bottom, defied statistics, silenced doubters and worked my way through the ranks to become an international thought leader; consultant, speaker, coach; recognized municipal government executive and an award-winning public administrator. Over my 22-year career, I've held 12 positions. Each was distinctly different than the last with varying skills required. I've raised three high school graduates who are now independent adults, all gainfully employed and responsible only for themselves. I am the audacity of hope now dedicated to showing others how to conquer obstacles and boldly thrive in leadership!

High Heel Leadership

"Leadership is about making others better as a result of your presence and making sure that impact lasts in your absence.".[2]

Sheryl Sanderberg, COO Facebook

I was about nine years old when I experienced my first pair of heels. They were patent leather white with a one-inch heel adorned by white ruffled socks that folded just under the ankle strap. I couldn't wait to walk in them and show off what was, for me, graduation day. I graduated from little girl to young lady. This day represented progress. My entire attitude shifted as I took my first step. I put one foot in front of the other and walked toward the door. Before I knew it my butt found its way to the floor, as if I were a newborn taking its very first steps. I quickly realized, while in a supine position, how much I'd underestimated this task. The same techniques used to go from arms to baby steps, would not work going from flats to heels. I had to relearn, retrain and rethink my approach, walking confidently in what had become unstable and unfamiliar territory. Determined not to be defeated, I did just that and achieved my goal.

There was additional growth with every inch added. I didn't just learn to walk, I mastered the art of walking in height, successfully. I eventually progressed from those one-inch heels to platforms of more than five-inches. Back straight, head high, attitude and confidence on steroids because I answered the challenge and was elevated. I had to reinvent myself, and gain the skills required, to walk in each increased level of elevation. This is high-heel leadership. Not the act of putting on, or wearing, a shoe. It is how we actively acquire, and then apply, improved techniques to reach every milestone toward our ascension to leadership. With every slipshod heel my form improved, fears subsided, doubts were removed and my internal voice strengthened. It renewed possibilities and awakened aspects of my untapped abilities.

High Heel Leadership, The Art of Being a Woman in Power explores the complex trials and stages of leadership and breaks down factors contributing to its struggles. As is true of all problems, solutions are possible when the right strategies are applied. The answers start with you. High heel leadership is about unraveling what stops you from unlocking your greatest leadership potentials, and unlearning those habits, while training you in the art of becoming a woman in power.

There is something majestic about a woman in a leadership role, especially when she commands the room, taking charge without permission, silently exuding strength and power. When you encounter her, you never forget.

How often have you been able to observe a woman in leadership? My first encounter came early in my career. During my first few days on the job, my supervisor introduced me to the team. I walked the halls shaking hands and receiving welcomes. We headed down the corridor that led to the offices of the organization's top administrators. I didn't know what to expect. When I saw her, I was pleasantly surprised. Her presence screamed powerhouse. Though small in stature, she appeared Goliath-like to me. I was drawn to her. I enthusiastically asked my supervisor, 'Who is that and how can I get to know her?' Ms. Johnson was the first female executive I'd meet. This encounter changed my life forever. She would, in time, become my direct report, my mentor, my confidant, my workplace fitness trainer and my cheerleader too.

From obtaining my undergraduate and graduate degrees, to purchasing my first home, her influence has resonated. For me, she was the epitome of high heel leadership. I thank God for her example, and the impact she continues to have, on my life.

I was once asked, 'Do women make good leaders and why?' My answer then, as now, 'Women make the best leaders. That does not minimize or downplay male leaders; but women infuse into their leadership specific, innate, skills that often don't come naturally to men. Soft skills, such as empathy, creativity, emotional and social awareness.'

My praise of women should not be misinterpreted as a feminist revolt against men in leadership. I celebrate the roles of strong men too. A strong man raised me. I have however, embraced the challenge to raise awareness, create change and offer solutions to, the stigmas that attach themselves to women in leadership. My intent is to edify women leaders, help to answer some of the questions they have asked themselves, and encourage every woman to speak about her accomplishments and capabilities without reservation. Women leaders are more likely to downplay their skills, and fail at self-promoting accomplishments and abilities, compared to their male counterparts. This leads, oftentimes, to stalled careers and has been found to contribute to gender pay gaps.

Christine Exley, an assistant professor at Harvard Business School, and Judd Kessler, associate professor at Wharton, conducted a research study to determine if gender differences in self-promotion exist and are a contributor to the negotiations, firm leadership and gender in earnings gaps. The study not only revealed that men engaged in substantially more self-promotion than women, despite equal study test performance, but the self-promotion paid off in increased earnings and job offers for those men.[3]

If you have a memorized script justifying why you shy away from openly acknowledging your achievements don't worry, you're not alone. It is difficult to know how much, or when, accomplishments and skills should be promoted. Cultural perception of cockiness, fear of career kills and women systemically conditioned to fill a certain role in society all contribute. I suspect however, that most women in leadership may not have had the fundamental support of more women encouraging self-promotion or advocating on their behalf.

Not to be mistaken as validation, the positive energy of one puissant woman to another can result in a synergy, a unification that propels all women to their next level of leadership. One thing's certain, we need to get clear about what prohibits self-promotion, learn to capitalize on every opportunity to self-promote and decide to champion for others when circumstances prevent someone from speaking on their own behalf.

Unity Among Women

I vividly remember the day I met one of the most trusted woman in my tribe. She was a political powerhouse with an impressive resume and experience to rival any male. For all of her accomplishments, and she had many, she was a humble, servant leader.

I met her after she was elected to her first four-year term. It was customary practice to pair seasoned staff with newly elected officials to acclimate them to the organization and help them transition into their role. We were both women of color with powerful mindsets and assertive personalities. Initially, I thought that would be a detriment but what seemed setup for failure turned into a Michael Jordan/Scottie Pippen-like combination!

Between us we formed a relationship of trust, loyalty, respect and accountability. This was the total opposite of what I, and others, were expecting. We learned how to work together, establishing a professional relationship that gave each of us the support we needed to excel. We didn't fight. In fact, our unity was so evident others began to take notice. We were both secure in our leadership roles and didn't need individual validation. When women are self-assured, self-validated and self-fulfilled, we can acknowledge the magic in one another without threat. This kind of self-awareness manifests into purpose-driven unification.

I needed that professional bond when I was unexpectedly appointed a director of human resources. The city manager was known for his unorthodox decision-making, but even I didn't see this one coming. I was shocked by the promotion but frankly, ready for the increased responsibilities. I quickly realized however, that not everyone shared our enthusiasm. The professional reinforcement I thought I had failed me. Everything I identified as safe, like my support group, and familiar, like my confidence, were questioned. I found myself battling to save my reputation and prove my qualifications. When an elected official publicly questioned and criticized my practical experience in the field, it was my Jordan/Pippen tribe member who openly advocated on my behalf.

Like many underestimated female leaders, I had the capacity to do well in this position. Though I couldn't check all the job description KSAs - knowledge, skills, and abilities - for the position, I had consistently demonstrated sound decision making with a record of successful, unconventional approaches to conflict resolution. These were some of the primary qualifications required. I knew that fighting the official's unsubstantiated opinion wouldn't have been the best decision for my career. Any uprising from me would have been seen as inappropriate and, quite possibly, used to legitimize his point. The Jordan to my Pippen became my voice. She firmly stood her ground in my defense. She made her position known by publicly stating:

"I believe Ms. Hampton is more than qualified to lead this department. You have men recently appointed in director positions that didn't have the experience or background in those areas; yet, they were deemed qualified and never questioned by this council. So why is it any different now for a woman, this woman?" [4]

Her advocacy turned things in my favor and strengthened my views on leadership. That experience, and others, steeled my resolve to be an avid supporter of other women. Now, I pay it forward.

Any leadership role is, to say the least, challenging, but when you can rely on the support of women to guide, advocate for and uplift you, that is true high heel leadership. The attacks are sure to come but, having a safe, supportive space makes even the fiercest storm easier to navigate.

"People throw rocks at things that shine."5 - lyric from Ours written by Taylor Swift.

As our station in life rises, we should always be prepared mentally, spiritually and emotionally for attacks intended to distract us from our goals and purpose. It is a guarantee of life you will be misunderstood, even ostracized, for the most insignificant of things. The day I was abruptly introduced to a local city resident was a reminder of this.

Shortly after returning home from speaking at an international conference, I came across this social media post (directly quoted without edits) that proved the point.

"It's already bad enough to keep Building Inspections straight but this has really left me disturbed since Tuesday!

Tuesday I had to make another trip down to the City Hall Building and while I was waiting to go through the metal detector and check in came in a woman all dolled up like she was stepping out of the VOGUE magazine with strong smells of Channel as she abruptly stopped looked at the police officer and walked right on up...no check in, no going through a metal detector just passing jail and heading to boardwalk as if she owned the darn monopoly! I questioned the police officer as I was up there on Friday and stated to the officer I believe my Mother Inlaw knows the lady that just walked by who was that and he said tgat was the City Manager's Sister and her name sir Oh that was Ms. CLAYTON! I thought well darn she gets the greenlight and I get the criminal treatment what makes her so damm special! I spoke to my husband and I google just the last name in Rocky Mount and saw how the onion was peeling back!

If Google is accurate then it states that Ms. CLAYTON isn't just a sister of the City Manager as the Officer of Rocky Mount stated but she is the ASSISTANT TO THE CITY MANAGER...ARE YOU SERIOUS FOLKS?!

In case you are wondering why there is so much confusion and corruption...GO FIGURE 6" red bottom stiletto's with plumes of perfume and forms of NEPOTISM is what our new figure heads are made about!

I just learned that even the Building Inspector is leaving the City due to this political arena!" [6]

You can only imagine the shock I experienced as I read, and reread, this outright character assassination. Was this stranger really talking about me? So many thoughts circled my mind. Did prejudice rear its ugly head this time aimed at me? Why was she so angry? What would make a woman erroneously judge me from such a brief encounter?

I don't think anyone can truly prepare for attacks, particularly if they are unwarranted. In this day of social media, many people hide behind their computers, blatherskite and spew hate without ever having to show their face. It's easy, and convenient, to think she was jealous and bothered by my style, but such thoughts aren't productive.

After more than twenty years in political and estrogen-charged environments I've learned the importance of self-preservation through preparation. My preparation starts with prayer, and ends with silent meditation. My mother gave me a strong spiritual foundation and I thank her for that. It has served me well. I have a strong faith that has guided, and helped, me in the toughest of times. My faith in a higher power made this, and other unflattering social media posts, bearable.

I am reminded of former President, Barack Obama's 2009 acceptance speech following the election. The rain was relentless as he made his way to the podium to address thousands in attendance and millions watching around the world. In this victorious, history-making, hard-fought moment he looked as if he was carrying the weight of the world on his shoulders. I believe he knew what should have been an auspicious occasion would not be long-lived. He knew the coming journey would not be easy, favorable, popular nor, despite the victory, wanted. He knew this pinnacle of American political leadership wasn't going to be a walk in the park; it wasn't a time to celebrate but, rather, to prepare.

I approach every career milestone with the question, *Okay Lord, what's next? How many more tests, how many more attacks, how must I prepare for this new journey?* It's probably this thought process that has kept me from becoming comfortable or complacent with a title, position or cush salary. The mindset of preparation is humbling and keeps me grounded. It also helps me to mentally assess potential issues in advance, preparing in a manner that will yield favorable and responsible resolutions. I take this same approach with everything in life. Remaining ready to face the day, and anything that comes along with it, challenges me to continue to develop and grow as a leader.

Growth As A Leader

Recalling the social media post, a few years prior I'm not sure how I would have handled it. More likely than not, I would have met fire with fire. Learning from my many experiences and listening to my mentors, as well as other women leaders, I chose instead to take the time to see past the fury and appeal to the spirit of togetherness I wish to see from every woman. I took a breath and responded with the artistry of a refined leader.

"Ms. C,

Women are amazing! We all are! I don't have to know you personally to appreciate your awesomeness by pure design. I've built my life, and career, supporting women in leadership because of our unique perspectives and resolve. Our strength, resilience and huge hearts allow us to win and to create winners. You can imagine then, my surprise to come across your post describing your perception of me as I walked, unknowingly, past you. I initially tried retracing my steps as I almost always speak to whomever I pass. I pay particular attention to women my senior, out of admiration and respect for the path they've paved for women like me to be able to hold office or sit at a boardroom table.

While I cannot, and will not, take responsibility for your perception of me, I can, and do, invite you to have lunch with me. Nothing breaks the ice like a good meal, and I'd appreciate hearing YOUR story. If your schedule doesn't permit, I'm a phone call away.

I pray that you receive this message as intended. More importantly, I pray the next time you see a woman who smells like Chanel, and looks as if she's just stepped out of Vogue magazine, you compliment her. You just may be saving her life!

Yours in Sisterhood,

Natasha"

My professional evolution enabled me to step outside of myself and see this woman as me. It feels empowering to see my growth as a leader. I have also come to understand that women can be, though unnecessarily, fearful of and intimidated by, other women in power.

Growth is a requirement of every leader. The ability to lead without being attached to the outcome is another. She never responded to my reply, but a response is not necessary for her self-examination and the realization of her power. Maybe she's ossified and rejects alternative perspectives. It's a position that she must reevaluate before she lashes out at another woman. Only then will she, or any of us, be able to choose the high road, as our former First Lady so eloquently stated.

True Leaders Are Servants

In my career I have always been able to tap into that inner power that drives me to do the best job possible and to exceed the expectations others have of me. I have learned many vital lessons about myself, and about how I lead a team. I fully understand and embrace the fact that I am a servant leader.

There have also been times that I have taken positions with the mindset that I needed to change things, that my purpose was to be the "savior." This approach, and false reality, often left me frustrated and exhausted. I stayed late hours to finish work that should, and could, have been handled by my team. I quickly learned that all great leaders must cultivate an environment for growth and unity within the group. I learned to listen to the needs of my staff. Their direct, and indirect, messages expanded my insight into emotional intelligence and its application.

From each position, I emerged with enhanced skillsets that allowed my leadership story to be written. Among the women, I recognized personal traits that I did not see in male counterparts. Women leaders worldwide are redefining leadership by rolling up their sleeves and doing the hard work it takes to build great organizations. As glycerin is to paint, I believe women activate workplaces, generating energy and encouraging engagement. According to Forbes, in 2015, Gallup research found that female managers are better at engaging employees (both male and female) than male managers.[7] This isn't to suggest that men aren't engaging leaders, rather it is a spotlight on a nontraditional leadership attribute known as interpersonal skills. A style of communication some may associate primarily as feminine.

I stand on the notion that women are transformative leaders. They bring a balance of emotion and logic to the decision-making process. We are balanced thinkers and, by default, problem solvers. When faced with crisis, we generally don't rush to resolve. We tend to think about problems, and their solutions, holistically to ensure all possibilities are considered, thus securing a better outcome for all involved.

Edie Weiner, President of Weiner, Edrich, Brown, Inc., a futurist consulting group, suggested in her keynote address that scientifically, women have a heightened ability to understand complex situations. She stated,

"Neuroscience, through brain imaging, is increasingly demonstrating the differences in the computational models of the male and female brain. The female brain, with its 10 to 20 million more connections in the corpus callosum connecting the left and right hemispheres, operates in a more integrated, parallel-processing mode, taking many more variables into account. This may make many women seem as if they are not efficiently focused on problems and solutions. But in actuality, they are effectively resolving problems and outcomes by looking at the 360-degree radius around the issue." [8]

The role of women in balancing and producing positive results in testosterone-driven workplaces are more apparent today than ever before because we can measure the change. Being able to measure this change provides critical data to support equal pay, leadership equity and to defeat disparity arguments.

Compassionate and Empathetic

According to information published by Psychology Today[9] empathy can be categorized in three ways:

"Cognitive: being able to know how the other person feels. Emotional: feeling what the other person feels. Sympathy: being ready to help someone in need."

Women often go beyond sympathy to seek an understanding of how others are feeling. It requires excellent discernment and close attention to the nuances of emotional signals. This skill allows for an ability to build judicious and empathetic interpersonal relationships.

Women Are Holistic Problem-Solvers

Women often take into consideration multiple, non-results-oriented, factors when problem-solving. They go about the business of understanding the social, mental, physical and emotional circumstances that created the issue. Looking beyond the - who, what, where, when, why and how – of a situation brings more effective, and lasting, results.

Women Build Strategic Alliances That Strengthen Organizations

No one company claims success and longevity without having had the good fortune of procuring resources and alliances. According to Gallup's survey [10] of more than eleven thousand people, women are far more effective at engaging and developing people, and more likely to build collaborative environments, than their male counterparts.

From small businesses to Fortune 500 conglomerates, the art of building connections and stimulating people are the main ingredients to any organization's success. More and more, decision makers are learning that a company's viability, and sustainability, are challenged without women at the helm who are building, connecting and strengthening the organization and its team.

Setting The Stage For Future Leaders

Throughout my career there were women that saw in me more than I saw in myself. From them I learned to stay surrounded by next-level thinkers, people who inspire me, the doers in our circle. Ms. Dorothy Pinder, my 8th-grade drama teacher, introduced me to the art of theater. She was a woman who saw something in me that I didn't see in myself. She cultivated what I had yet to discover. She made me believe that I could captivate an audience and hold them in a room, for as long as I desired, simply by the way I projected words! From 8th grade, and throughout my college career, that knowledge inspired me. It also prepared me for leadership in government all because a teacher/leader/woman nurtured, appreciated and embraced my talents.

When I started my career in public service, it was the mentorship of a woman who stressed the importance of going back to school. She challenged me to embrace a vision for my life. After obtaining my undergraduate degree, it was yet another woman that insisted I continue with post-secondary education. This is the effect women have on one other. Women leaders pushed me to show up big and be proud.

These women really did set the stage for me as a future leader. They showed me that leadership is about making others better as a result of your presence, and the impact that you can have on those lives.

Our work produces undeniable results that promote others to stand in their own power. Throughout this book I will dispel myths that surround women, and women in leadership. I want to include you in the dialogue, not just toss a lot of facts and figures at you. You deserve the opportunity to have an opinion on the subject. I welcome an open dialogue from you after you complete the book. Effective leadership is a two-way conversation and there is so much more to be uncovered on this topic.

HIGH HEEL REFLECTIONS:

- ❖ Become an advocate for women leaders.

- ❖ Self-preservation begins with preparation.

- ❖ Attacks are to be taken in stride but never personally.

- ❖ Leaders are servants first.

- ❖ It is our responsibility to set the stage for future leaders.

Questions:

✓ Are you practicing self-preservation? If so, how? If not, what will you do to start?

_____

_____

_____

✓ What is your reaction when someone questions your qualifications?

_____

_____

_____

✓ How are you paving the way for future leaders?

_____

_____

_____

High Heel
Leadership
is Discovery

REDEFINING LEADERSHIP: WHAT IS LEADERSHIP, REALLY?

"The way a man thinketh in his heart, so is he." Proverbs 23:7

The big day I had been anxiously anticipating for over five months had finally arrived. I was nervous to say the least. You would have thought I was being considered for an Academy Award. With sweaty palms and butterflies in my stomach, I anxiously waited for the announcement to be made. The very excitement of being chosen to fill a coveted position was here. It was my time! For years I dreamed of climbing the corporate ladder. For the first time I would be able to see my vision come to fruition. I had often thought about what it would be like to stop living paycheck-to-paycheck. It wasn't about the material status, it was about being a better caregiver and role model to my kids.

I was a single mother of three, the sole provider for my family. I was thankful for the opportunity. It couldn't have come at a better time in my life. The raise in pay and additional benefits were only some of what I needed. This was a step on my career path, a step toward advancing my future.

I questioned myself for weeks. *Am I good enough? Will they really promote me? Am I ready?* I knew I deserved the position but wondered if the position recruiter did too. I eventually stopped entertaining those negative thoughts, pulled myself together, envisioned how I would raise the bar and surpass all expectations. I admit I couldn't wait to decorate my new office too.

That day, everything around me felt different. I felt good about myself as I began to reflect on my journey but waiting for the announcement was nerve wrecking. All I could do was sit and wait for what I optimistically anticipated as good news in my *old* office. I decided to get up and walk past my *new* office.

I caught a glimpse of someone sitting at *my* new desk. Of all the things I'd imagined happening that morning, I never expected this.

A strange woman was sitting there taking notes while my supervisor stood over her. *Who is she and why is she sitting in my new office?* I thought, *She's using my new desk, sitting in my new chair.* I hadn't seen this woman before. I was puzzled. It was an unwritten policy of the organization to promote from within so I knew she couldn't be the new hire. *Keep a straight face Natasha. Maybe you're overthinking this,* my thoughts continued. *Breathe Natasha. Maybe she's just organizing things for you.*

I was wrong. Obviously, for one reason or another, the policy had been overlooked. My heart sank. I was at a loss for words. My eyes filled with tears. It felt like I had been punched in the stomach. Every part of my body tensed. I froze. I didn't know what to do.

Later that morning I tried to keep my composure, as best I could, when introduced to the new employee taking my, rightly deserved, position. *Wait a minute. This isn't fair! She's not an internal hire. This is wrong. That position was mine.* I began contemplating my next steps. Should I express my disappointment in what, I felt, was selective use of policy or better yet, go straight to the CEO through a board member with whom I'd developed a great working relationship? I thought long and hard, getting angrier by the minute.

I ultimately realized no matter how angry and betrayed I felt, no matter how much I had prepared for the job, no matter how unfair I felt I had been treated by the system of selective policy use, I had to face the reality that nothing in corporate America is guaranteed.

It was also a time to reflect on what I'd learned from observing successful leaders and the advise of my mentors. I had to decide if acting out of anger as a result of this disappointing experience would be my unsung leadership story. I made the decision to thrive, despite a setback, and to show up like leaders often do.

I chose to congratulate and welcome the newest member of the team and wholeheartedly support her as needed.

A couple months later, the same position opened in a different department. One of the people who had interviewed me for the other position was now the head of this department. He reached out and offered me the very position I thought had slipped away. Moreover, the assignment location would give me the opportunity to learn a new area of discipline and created the visibility that eventually led to my first appointment to senior management.

High heel leadership is the art of learning that, while every battle may be worth fighting, it's not in your best interest to engage in an all-out war. Thoroughly examine every situation with foresight on eventual outcomes.

Since that day more than fifteen years ago now, many things have changed. I have had the honor to serve in various capacities and in roles that led to other opportunities for advancement in my career. I have managed multi-billion dollar budgets for fast-growing and redeveloping municipalities in both South Florida and North Carolina. I have traveled around the world sharing my experiences in, and knowledge of, municipal government. I've evolved as a female leader in a male-dominated sector.

Perhaps the most satisfying part of the journey has been the many women I continue to meet. They ask me the hard questions about leadership, and life. I am obligated to tell them my truth. I started at the bottom and I pushed my way to the top. I had the support of strong, successful, women and men who embraced, and guided, me as I sought out and realized my own success.

Establishing myself as a female leader hasn't always been easy. As I grew professionally, I also grew personally. Each new role challenged me to think in new ways. They forced me to fully understand the organizations, and people, I served. These new opportunities came with a sense of responsibility to create, promote and advocate for parity for other women, offering positions in leadership within these organizational structures.

I have always believed that whenever we are afforded greater opportunity, we must leave the door open for others to walk through, then inspire them to set a blueprint for their own success. For women in the workplace, this is most important. I learned this from women throughout my career who graciously helped and inspired me.

The face of leadership is evolving, especially the role of women in organizations across America and abroad. Acceptance in the boardroom, political office and C-suite positions such as chief operating officer, chief executive officer and chief financial officer, are finally becoming more commonplace. Nearly a third of global S&P 500 boards include three or more women growing from 19% in 2015 to 29% in 2018.[11] Marjorie Scardino became the first woman appointed to the board of Twitter in 2013 and Ngozi Okonjo-Iweala, a former finance minister of Nigeria, was appointed to the board of Twitter in 2019. Facebook's appointment of Chief Operating Officer Sheryl Sandberg was a continued step toward increasing the number of C-Suite positions held by women.

Women also showed strong representation in the 2018 United States elections. This advancement in political office was historic with women holding 21% of the seats in the House of Representatives, a 4.1% increase from 2016 and 23%, an increase of 1%, in the Senate. At this moment, Congress has the most women serving at once in U.S. history.[12] Deb Haaland and Sharice Davids became the first Native American women elected to Congress. Rashida Tlaib and Ilhan Omar the first Muslim women to represent their states in the House. Alexandria Ocasio-Cortez and Abby Finkenauer are the youngest women ever elected to Congress.

As roles of acceptable leadership are redefined, so too are the expected behaviors associated with those roles. Boardroom banter and corporate politics that have been long associated with how a woman should appear and conduct herself at the regulated, and highly coveted, "big table" are increasingly eroding. What I espouse here may seem controversial to some. To others it may be welcomed and long overdue. Nevertheless, it is my goal to challenge societal biases on leadership both in terms of how it's defined and cultivated.

I want you to understand that leadership doesn't start with a title, position, salary or any other tangibles. Leadership begins with belief in yourself and knowing that you have the skills to lead. I often wonder, had I realized this sooner, if the journey to my seat at the boardroom table would have been less challenging?

What Is Leadership; Really?

Simply stated, leadership is an attitude. It starts with YOU! It's essential to rethink what leadership means. Titles don't define leaders, neither do socioeconomic status or pay. It is not the name on the office door or the latest headline news.

Any woman, at any time, can realize her value and decide to lead no matter the role she serves within an organization. She can lead from every position and should think of herself as a leader. You should be thinking about leading even at the beginning of your career. You can't grow or ascend to the kind of leader an organization needs if you aren't considering its future and your role in that structure. If you wait until you obtain a title to develop the attributes of leadership, you'll become a manager. Managers manage work. Managing work is not leadership.

Before I started my public sector career, I worked a few different jobs. I remember applying for an executive position working alongside the vice president of a high-profile construction company. I was professional in every way and possessed the skills to do the job. I was confident this was the position for me. I went through the orientation and aced the interview. All seemed to be going my way. Then, I was asked my desired annual salary. I thought about that question for a moment and said, matter of factly, 'Well, I'd like no less than $8 an hour.' I was ultimately offered a receptionist position.

According to what many textbooks suggested, I dressed professionally, obtained the skills for the job I wanted and I was personable, relatable too. Why didn't I get the job I applied for? What was I missing? There's a saying that I use when coaching my teams for optimum productivity – 'Think it, and so it shall be!'

The one thing I didn't have was the mindset. I didn't think leadership, I thought employment. I didn't see myself as a leader, especially in an assistant position. The interviewer asked for my salary request and I undersold myself, lowering my value. I thought I was playing it safe but I had discounted my worth. Why would this company see any value in me when I undervalued myself? What a painful but critical lesson to learn.

When I began to understand this principle, I committed to helping women who didn't see themselves as essential. I helped them realize the importance of their role, relative to the success of the organization, and how to leverage those skills for advancement. It was a concept that I personally tested as I transitioned from one position to the next.

With a passion to mentor, I initiated women empowerment and award recognition programs to celebrate women and honor front-line employees. It was vital for me to encourage the recognition of staff so that they, and others, could realize their leadership potential. It boosted the morale of the women,

Natasha S. Hampton

and anyone who had felt unappreciated, allowing them to see a bright future for themselves.

"A leader takes people where they want to go. A great leader takes people where they don't necessarily want to go, but ought to be." -Rosalynn Carter[13]

The Transformation Of Female Leadership

Quite a bit has changed since 1990 when Sally Helgesen wrote her groundbreaking book, *The Female Advantage: Women's Ways of Leadership.*[14] Helgesen intentionally refrained from using terms such as female or woman leader. In her view, these terms create barriers, conjuring up old assumptions, practices and language that can become hurdles to equal access. Today, we openly acknowledge and celebrate women leaders by that precise title. We do so in spite of the fantastic strides women have made in business since 1990. Barriers, including unequal pay, unconscious bias and too few leadership positions, remain, debunking Helgensen's theory by their mere presence. The fight continues. Creating opportunities for women to lead remains the priority.

As a woman serving in executive leadership, I have found it important to help other women offering solutions, as well as comprehensive strategies, to address issues they may face in their careers and relationships. It is always my intention to invoke intelligent conversation and uncover gray areas. These are the spots often overlooked in relation to how women in leadership should, and are expected to, perform. These are the criteria upon which women in leadership are judged. Often cited as the reason for lack of women in

37

leadership roles is the lack of support from their male counterparts. Regularly overlooked and unspoken is the tearing down of women in leadership at the hands of other women. Cattiness and outright sabotage among women has, in part, continued because we haven't branded our own image of cooperative leadership. We'll address this further in chapter six.

Effective Leadership

It's always challenging to address the topic of leadership because, truthfully, not everyone in a leadership position is an effective leader. There is an art to effective leadership. It should be analyzed, presented, defined and fine-tuned, then used to instruct up-and-coming leaders and implemented daily by those currently in leadership roles. Great leaders should lead to bring about change in a culture, environment and organization when needed.

I was once asked why I wanted to be a director. I answered, 'Because, I'm a leader!' The question that followed was, 'Yes, but why do you want to lead?' I was hesitant to respond. I didn't want to sound pompous. My supreme confidence took over however and I said, 'You have many who think they are leaders. They strut around and boast about their position, status and accomplishments, but it's almost always superficial. I am a leader because I lead with balance, intention, fairness, care, deliberation, collaboration, thought and a zeal to empower others. Most often, I do it quietly. I am a leader people follow because I've been where they are and, hopefully, am an example of what they can aspire to become.'

I knew at that moment that driving change through leadership was my calling. I now understand that leaders must accept the responsibility of serving others. It is the first step to becoming an effective leader. If more leaders realized this, their policies would be far more effective. Oh, how they could then expand their expectations.

Confidence is not only necessary but instrumental for effective leadership. Not to be mistaken for arrogance, confident leaders are trustworthy and capable. That combination is what creates certainty. People gravitate toward certainty because change is hard to manage, both personally and professionally.

"Teetering leadership: Being confident but not overconfident. When it comes to leadership, one important consideration is the kind of leader people are willingly to follow. An authentic leader with confidence is important to followers." - International City/County Management Association (ICMA) SmartBrief publication.[15]

It is time to unlearn traditional methods of leadership, such as influence can only be demonstrated based on title identification; or leaders are born because of perceived natural abilities; or only certain position holders in an organization should make decisions, usually those with titles. These, and others, have proven ineffective yet continue to be passed down all the same.

There needs to be a better understanding of the dynamics of people and what makes them want to be led. More specifically, what motivates them to be led by women? Over my career I have honed my ability to connect with people because I have found that people follow those to whom they feel connected. I have come to recognize that connection must be authentic, not some contrived sense of caring. Effective leadership is the ability to tap into the needs of people, to earnestly engage, and to work toward solutions that permanently change lives.

Establishing trust is a significant component of effective leadership. It can only be done if the leader is willing to build substantive relationships. Leadership is not self-serving. My leadership style consists of fair and collaborative, solution-based strategy development, created in a culture of trust. One of the biggest pieces of advice I can give to those in leadership, and those striving toward it, is to stay true to, and authentic in, your selfless leadership purpose!

The Ugly Side Of Leadership

It's inevitable that you will experience the ugly side of leadership. If I had a dollar for every time my ability or decision-making was questioned by subordinates, co-workers, managers and elected officials, regardless of gender, I could retire today, filthy rich and living off the dividends.

There are people who want to be in your position but don't want to do the work you did to earn the right. People often take on positions without clearly understanding that it's not just the glory that comes along with the title. There is work you need to be prepared to gracefully handle. That includes all the negative things that come with the territory. How you manage is important.

I remember when I was preparing for the launch of the Let's Move! initiative created by former First Lady Michelle Obama. I'd stepped up to develop, and lead, the event. There was a lot of time and effort put into coordinating the visit. My team and I worked tirelessly together strategizing, organizing and orchestrating every aspect to ensure a flawless launch. We were 48 hours away. Everyone was super excited about the details surrounding the First Lady's appearance.

Then, seemingly out of nowhere, questions began to surface concerning why I was in charge. Why had individual decisions been made and were the "right" people advised. In the final hours, everyone wanted to claim the event as their own. The background noise they created was nearly deafening. They wanted to swoop in for some glory.

It became disheartening as well as distracting. In that moment, the best piece of advice I received was to block out the noise, remain focused on the event's purpose and see it through. That helped me put my attention where it was needed and is why I passionately supported the initiative.

When contemplating your career's next level ask yourself, Why? If your answer doesn't include changing the lives of others for the better, creating opportunities so that others may empower themselves, interrupting the status quo or a willingness to confront issues plaguing communities, your leadership goals will be short-lived. Your effectiveness is already compromised because leadership requires a heart-check.

You must constantly ask yourself if you are focusing on the right thing. Is your heart in the right place? Are you doing this for others? Do you seek the best possible outcome? If you can answer yes to those questions then block out the noise, keep moving forward and watch your effective leadership blossom. The event was a success, absent the First Lady who was unable to attend. The community was encouraged to take responsibility for their health and actions, a challenge that will affect them for generations to come. The 'why' of your actions should always be bigger than the 'who' and 'what.' The vehicle you use to initiate the change doesn't matter. A genuine leader wants to see everyone win.

Barriers Still Exist

For women, there are barriers that continue to plague our advancement. Paramount are the few leadership opportunities available in the workplace. When assuming leadership roles, or ascending any organizational structure, women must work to create thoughtful policies. Programs that foster and encourage leadership development for women help your organization. Identifying, designing and implementing career ladders is just one of many ways to begin the eradication of workplace toxicity for women.

It's time we have a good look at our intentions, both good and bad, and create a safe space for women to talk about and develop solutions. There are plenty of books, and a lot of commentary, on women in leadership.

It's time women set some rules and redefined expectations. I am confident women will conquer present and future barriers, crafting a blueprint for other women to garner their strength, and their voice, in their own rise to power. Being a forerunner is never a glorified position. It's tough, thankless and spirit weakening, but the sweet taste of accomplishment is undeniable.

I often ponder the legacy I'd like to leave to this world. Although I have made many advancements, some of which we will discuss, I would most like to create a legacy of recognizing gaps in our systems and daring to build bridges; bridges that innovatively create pathways for the global advancement of women.

HIGH-HEEL REFLECTIONS

❖ Leadership is an attitude that starts with you.

❖ Help others by offering solutions as well as comprehensive strategies.

❖ Leaders should lead to bring about change to a culture, environment or an organization.

❖ Your why should include changing the lives of others, creating opportunities, interrupting the status quo and being willing to confront issues plaguing communities.

Questions:

✓ How have you effectively brought about change to your organization's culture and/or environment?

_____

_____

_____

✓ Do you often question your capability or capacity as a leader? If yes, in what ways can you begin to build your confidence?

_____

_____

_____

✓ In the past year, what actions have you taken to affect change in your community?

_____

_____

_____

High Heel
Leadership
is Clear

FINDING YOUR VOICE AS A LEADER

"I come from a people who have struggled and died in order to have a voice in this country, and I refuse to be muzzled." [16]-

Oprah Winfrey

When the head of my department asked me to join him for, what I perceived as an after-hours business meeting, I thought nothing of it. After all he was a leader in the organization, one that everyone admired for his business acumen. The company culture made it normal for colleagues to work well past business hours on projects. That night however, felt different. As we approached valet service anxiety kicked in. *I'm in trouble* I thought, realizing there was nowhere to turn. Not long after that business meeting (clearly a date for him) the bi-weekly floral deliveries, uninvited visits to my home, and offers of large sums of money (which I did not accept) began to interrupt our working relationship. Rumors began to circulate that I was having an inappropriate sexual relationship with him. Things were quickly spinning out of control.

The truth was I was innocent, naive and afraid. At the time, the situation was way more than I could, or should, have had to handle, especially as a single mother. *Should I speak up?* I thought to myself. *No, I can't afford to lose my job,* I reasoned. No one asked me what was happening. According to rumors this was the reason I was progressing in the organization. I quietly dealt with the shame while inside I wanted to scream out and speak my truth. Where was my voice? Why didn't I say something? How could I let this happen? I had convinced myself that I had somehow done something wrong.

Unsure of how I should handle the situation, I reached out to my circle for guidance. With the help of one of my confidants, I was able to mitigate these unsolicited advances. After allowing me to vent, cry and scream, I was instructed to go purchase a Father's Day-type card and write.

"I want to thank you for your mentorship. You're like a father figure to me. I appreciate the opportunity to have a professional relationship with you and work together toward the organization's goals."

I had no idea if this would work but it was much better than the ideas I had. They would surely have landed me in prison or, at best, on the unemployment line. I accepted her counsel and did as she advised.

Such a burden was lifted off me emotionally that day. I will never forget how empowered I felt when I finally stood up for myself. I encourage every woman to find her voice and recognize the power they have, especially when they are being violated. His advances didn't entirely stop but, by acting immediately, things became much easier to handle.

I wish I could tell you that it did the trick the first time but, after a few more returned gifts to sway my position, I repeated the guidance provided and he finally got the picture. While this was not the rise-up, power-to-the-people solution you may have expected, my sister/mentor/confidant helped me to recognize just how powerful a voice I have. By asking for help handling the situation, I was able to redirect a potentially career-ending course. I found an untapped dimension of voice called strategy.

This happened many years ago, but it prompted me to be an advocate for other women as they find their own voice. This was just one of the many experiences I endured. Others included learning how to be confident in my skin and learning how to adjust to other women leaders.

In general, women are often subjected to workplace sexual harassment. Women of color however are more likely to be targeted. "Statistics confirm that sexual harassment is alive and well across all industries—and women of color working low-wage jobs are facing the brunt of this abuse," said Emily Martin, Vice President for Education & Workplace Justice at the National Women's Law Center. Women of color are less likely to be acknowledged, either as victims or advocates. USA Today reports,[17] "Though the #metoo hashtag was created by a black woman more than a decade ago, the faces of the cause have often been white and affluent."

What should a woman that finds herself in a #metoo situation do? For centuries she had two options, (1) Report the incident to human resources fearing that she may lose her job, be retaliated against or never have advancement opportunities; or (2) Play along hoping that accepting his advances will prove beneficial to her long-term career aspirations. These are not viable options in the 21st century.

Conversations must be had. More women must rise to power. This is not a problem that will go away because we take the lead at the current rate of 6.6% of Fortune 500 companies.[18] Exposing predators doesn't account for all the people behind the offender who allow the bad behavior to continue. Be a leader from where you are today. If you see something, say something. Exposing the problem is a definite step in the right direction and that is 100% within your power.

Your Voice Is Oxygen

Your voice is a powerful instrument of self-awareness, advocacy and change. It's the space in which you dwell. I like to describe your voice as oxygen. Breathing becomes increasingly harder without a steady and even flow of oxygen. Oxygen gives you life. It's an unassuming force generously woven into every fiber of your being that ultimately makes you who you are. Your voice is life; it's your power! It has the ability to build sustainable foundations and change lives. Thinking about your voice as simply a tool of speech is a mistake. Your voice must be cultivated, protected and celebrated. It is what defines your unique qualities.

My experience caused me to question the strength and value of my voice. It took some time, years in fact, before I felt confident enough to speak up. If you have ever struggled to find your voice, then you know how frustrating it can be.

Your voice is the light that reveals the true essence of your being. A flickering light is irritating. It is unsteady and erratic. A steady light, one that shines bright, makes it easier for someone to see. Be seen!

Women often have an internal conflict concerning how brightly to let their light shine. They engage a dimmer switch, downplaying their abilities and allowing men to dominate the areas where they may not feel best qualified. They take on roles of lesser responsibility, shrinking back when they should allow their light to illuminate their path forward. I am not claiming that discovering your true voice is easy. For many women it is a life-long journey.

Can Anyone Hear Me?

Finding your voice starts with recognizing the barriers that may have been placed on you very early in life. Were you told young ladies are to be seen and not heard; little girls don't speak like that; don't talk back; or simply, shhh? These experiences, while well-intended, may have shaped the way you think about your voice and your power. From a very early age women are often taught to suppress their voice and that speaking up is not lady-like. It's not surprising then that many women find it difficult to find their voice, especially in male-dominated spaces. It's also not surprising that once we find our voice we refuse to ever be silenced again. The sad reality is that many women never find the inner voice. In a world that may want to silence conflict, it is no doubt the ones that speak up who will make history.

"The most courageous act is still to think for yourself. Aloud."-
Coco Chanel[19]

Did you know your appearance alone speak volumes for you and can determine how others hear you? I don't mean if you're wearing designer clothes or carrying a fancy handbag. In the opening of Beyonce's *Crazy in Love* video, she's seen walking toward the camera, back straight, eyes focused, shoulders squared, mesmerizing. Your first thoughts are fierce, confident, strong, powerful and capable. All of that, and she doesn't speak a syllable.

Your appearance is also your voice, and people often decide who you are without hearing a word you say. For a long time I would walk with my head down. Not because I lacked confidence. In fact, I wasn't even aware I was doing it. A colleague approached me as I was walking back to my office with my head down and asked, 'Why are you walking like that? Is something wrong?' Of course, I said no but she followed that with, 'I noticed that is something you often do. That sends me mixed messages.' Puzzled by her observation I asked, do what? She said, 'You walk with your head down a lot.' I said, 'I wasn't aware I was doing that. But how does that send you mixed messages?' She replied, 'I don't believe you lack confidence but when I see you walking with your head down, I'm not sure if your confidence comes and goes, or if you're simply pretending to have it in the first place.' Whoa! I thought long and hard about that. What I concluded was my voice is nonverbal and can be heard in the way I present myself.

People determine several things about you within a matter of minutes. The employees you supervise will do the same. Is she trustworthy? Is she capable? Is she a leader I can support and follow? So what is your appearance saying to others? If you aren't sure, select a person you know will be honest with you and ask, what does my appearance say about me?

Have a talk with yourself and analyze where you are in the process of finding your voice.

Ask yourself these questions:

❖ Who am I?

❖ What does my voice say about me?

❖ Does my voice represent who I am and/or who I want to be?

❖ What do I need to adjust to create the sound that represents me?

You should sit down with a few trusted confidants and share what you discover in your self-analysis. Ask if they too shared those impressions. If they did, how do those initial impressions match their more developed understanding of who you are now that they have spent time with you? Juxtapose what you've learned, from how others hear you, with how you'd like to be heard.

The Evolution of your Voice

It's not presumptuous to think that your voice will, and should, evolve with you. Your voice is not just what you say, it's the way you carry yourself when you walk into a room. It's the way you show up when you sit at the boardroom table. Whether spoken aloud or through gesture, it's important to learn when, and how, to use it. Through my experience with sexual harassment, I learned that my voice comes in many forms and is sometimes guided by trusted confidants. It's vital to uncover your voice before you are faced with a situation that damages your reputation, brand or career.

Sometimes women in leadership are confused about how to boldly show up as a leader in a room. Former Secretary of State Madeline Albright in a September 2017 Time interview[20] said,

"I have often been the only woman in the room and I thought to myself, 'Well, I don't think I'll say anything today because it'll sound stupid,' and then some man says it and everyone thinks it's brilliant and you think, 'Why didn't

I talk?' If we are in a meeting, we're there for a reason. The bottom line is if you're only there, not speaking you kind of create the impression that you're not prepared to be there."

I have watched women function, almost to the point of confusion, as they attempted to be all things, including silent. Rather than define their voice and stay true to themselves, they imitate what they've seen or heard and regurgitate thoughts that are totally unauthentic and uncharacteristic. Although very comfortable in my skin today, I can vividly remember the times when I wasn't sure who I was. As many women are taught to 'know their place', and encouraged to 'stay in your lane', it's a natural response.

There was a noticeable evolution in my voice as I became unapologetic about my purpose in life. Mixing the ideologies that you are taught as a young girl, with the realities of a woman in power, may muddy waters for some. You may even ask how do I mix both worlds? As a child you're taught to be quiet. In the boardroom, you must speak up.

The evolution of your voice is a process. It takes time, patience and acceptance. One of the many stages of evolution you will endure is cultivating your voice. As your voice evolves, you are able to stand firm in your position and speak your truth. There will come a time, if it has not already, where everything you stand for will be tested. Do you compromise yourself for the good of others or do you stand firm, unwavering in your principles? There is no right or wrong answer to this question. Only you get to define your voice in those moments. How much, and at what pace your voice evolves, is completely up to you.

Trust the process of becoming. With time, we all change. The true you is ever-evolving. Adjust your voice accordingly. You're not the same person you were ten years ago.

Man, Oh Man, Oh Woman

There may come times when you even question if your femininity must take a back seat to the position. Christa Quarles, CEO of OpenTable, the world's largest provider of online restaurant reservations, said,

"When I first started my career, I was working in a male-dominated office, and I felt that I needed to show up as a man to be accepted by men. I thought my voice needed to sound like a man's voice so that I would be included. I felt that if I wasn't included if I didn't laugh at their inappropriate comments and jokes - spoke too soon or complained then I wouldn't get ahead. My realization wasn't an overnight thing. It was a slower evolution that grew as I gained more power and became a leader. Leaders have to step forward and say, This matters, and I'm going to do something about it."[21]

I too believe that you can be in the room with men and maintain your femininity. As women, we must learn how to unapologetically, authentically, embrace the qualities that define us. This will dispel the myths that leadership comes wrapped in a pinstripe suit and necktie! Thinking you can't properly lead in a pencil skirt and stilettos is archaic. How you present yourself, within tasteful guidelines, should not factor into an evaluation of your ability to effectively function as a leader.

Maintaining Your Voice With Women Of Power

Sadly, there will be instances where other women will advocate for your downfall. No matter where you are on your career path you need to think strategically about how to make your voice heard. When dealing with women in power, 'I have to let these women know who I am, or they need to acknowledge my credentials' is the wrong approach because you are trying to prove that you belong. When unsettled nerves cause you to question whether you're recognized there is no need to speak. The fact that you are in the room is your validation. Always keep your emotions, and ego, in check. Think about filling the space you occupy, wherever that is, without screaming you belong.

The Power In Being Silent

Have you ever heard the phrase silence is golden? That's because it is! I have been in male-majority meetings and not uttered a word. My choice to speak, or not, was determined by the outcome sought. In other words, if I wanted a particular answer or a solution in my favor, I would use my voice to persuade the outcome. Otherwise, I intently listened!

Women leaders realize that being in the room, sitting at the table is, by itself, voice. When there are situations that call for you to speak up do so with power, grace and authority. Just be sure to speak in such a way that it doesn't preclude another from having the opportunity to do the same. As women at the table, we have options. Our focus should not be so self-serving that we neglect the women that are coming behind us, however. What we do at the coveted table as a choice, is a consequence others will feel. Silence doesn't mean you are less powerful. Sometimes it exhibits that you are more powerful than they may have recognized.

Leading with the grace, beauty and the effectiveness of a quiet storm is a skill that few have mastered. How many of you were told as a little girl, while wearing your cute white ruffle socks, lace dress and curly hair with pink bows, to sit with your legs crossed in the corner and speak only when spoken to? Meanwhile, you watched boys play loudly, speak abruptly and yell while wearing their Sunday best. For me this was a little confusing. I later realized just how much of a learning moment it was. While sitting still I was able to organize thoughts, contemplate options, determine consequences. In business this is known as a strengths, weaknesses, opportunities and threats (SWOT) analysis. These stages are traits of effective leadership that we unassumingly learned very early. Maybe 'Shhh, be seen and not heard!' wasn't so bad after all! Being silent, however, has its limits.

The Importance Of Using Your Voice

When you have not yet grasped the importance of telling your story you give others permission to narrate it for you. You may suffer emotional, mental and physical abuse as a result. There were times when I allowed my voice to be silenced for the sake of a relationship. Expecting my third child, my partner at the time introduced two significant changes into my life, a new faith and another pregnant woman. Don't worry, this book is called *High Heel Leadership* not *How to Get Away with Murder*. He was not the father of the woman's child. My partner agreed to help his friend, who had asked if his pregnant girlfriend could stay with us.

I gave birth to a healthy, 9 lb. 14 oz., baby boy but it was a very challenging delivery. Postpartum depression (PPD) took over. I was caring for a teenager, toddler and a newborn in a three-bedroom apartment. Now I had PPD, a woman I barely knew, and a partner I didn't like very much to contend with too. I was overworked, tired, frustrated and unhappy but said nothing. That suffering in silence went on for too long. One evening I sat in my car with two bottles of prescription drugs. I wanted what I was feeling to end; I wanted to die.

That night my internal voice, which is rooted in my faith, spoke to me. It averted what could have been a tragic situation. I was blessed. I do realize my story isn't isolated. Mine is not the outcome for many leaders accustomed to being strong for others. The pressures and expectations we put on our own lives, to help others, leaves us without the wherewithal to self-help. This weakens the best of leaders. It also leaves leaders unaccustomed to expressing their own needs to others.

I share my truth for a few reasons. First, to show just how important it is for a woman, young or old to find their voice. Secondly, if you are a woman that has found your voice, helping others to find theirs should be your organon. Lastly, no matter where life takes you, as a leader you can always find your voice. You can always rewrite your story.

HIGH HEEL REFLECTIONS

❖ Your voice is your oxygen. It is a pure instrument of self-awareness, advocacy and change.

❖ Your voice is a light revealing the true essence of your being.

❖ When you fail to grasp the importance of telling your own story, you give others permission to write it for you.

❖ Finding your voice starts with recognizing the barriers that have been placed on you early in life and eradicating them.

❖ Women leaders should realize that being in the room and sitting at the table, by itself, is a voice.

Questions:

✓ Do you understand the difference between having a voice and speaking?

_____

_____

_____

✓ Have you started the journey to finding your voice?

_____

_____

_____

✓ Does your voice represent you?

_____

_____

_____

✓ Is your voice responsible?

_____

_____

_____

✓ What will you do to develop your voice?

_____

_____

_____

High Heel
Leadership
is Evolution

In the Absence of Fear and Doubt

"When I dare to be powerful, to use my strength in the service of my vision, then it becomes less and less important whether I am afraid." [22] Audre Lorde

While climbing the ladder of success, I sometimes felt that I wasn't good enough. There were always questions. Am I supposed to be here? Do I have what it takes? Is what I bring to the table valuable enough? In my self-discovery process I learned that I was always where I should be. It didn't matter if the woman or man sitting across the table had more experience or a higher degree. I eventually realized that the fears, exampled above, had been guiding my path, both professionally and personally, in unacceptable ways.

When I found out I was pregnant at seventeen, it was the first time I understood disappointment. I felt alone. That was probably the first time I silenced my voice in fear of what my parents would say, and how others would perceive me. There was a stigma that followed girls that became pregnant young and out of wedlock. Without knowing it, I had bought into the lies. As a result, I hid my pregnancy from my parents until five days after giving birth. Fear has a way of affecting our emotions and, oftentimes, appears as shame.

I decided, in fear, that I would try and figure it out on my own. Fear stifles you. It stops you from moving forward. I feared what having a child young would do to my life. I made decisions based on those fears. I was raised in a strict household where my mother was a devout Jehovah's Witness and my father, a skilled corporal-punishment practitioner. Based on those experiences, and the lessons they provided, I convinced myself that my family wouldn't support me. I stopped believing in love and compassion. Fear can create mental barriers that can be difficult to overcome.

Today I ask the better, answerable, question. The question that leads to solutions: What are you afraid of?

Fear and doubt show up in many forms: procrastination, distraction, laziness and self-sabotage are among them. I am sure I'm not too different from many other women when it comes to being nervous about the unknown. I can remember the butterflies in my stomach every time I challenged myself to achieve the next highest goal. Writing this book was no exception.

It's important for you to understand, and recognize, that fear is not a spiritual emotion. In the presence of fear, doubt ensues. Without addressing the fear, the doubt will derail your destiny of power and leadership. Your choice to read this book is not coincidental. If you get clear about fear and doubt, and what place they have in your life, then you can step out of fear's shadow and exercise faith in yourself to do the things that make you whole.

I now understand that fear is simply false evidence appearing real (FEAR).[23] I didn't always know this. For most of my young adult life, fear guided my decisions, relationships and actions. My pregnancy and sexual harassment are two examples of how I questioned my uniqueness and beauty based on how I perceived someone else would respond. Fear and doubt have no place in your space.

From A Test To Attest

I spoke earlier about being accused of having an inappropriate relationship with a male colleague. The accusations resurfaced amid a demand by his director, and eventually my immediate supervisor, to terminate him based on allegations of theft. A fifteen year, otherwise exemplary, employee was being fired for admittedly taking a potted plant from the back of a company utility vehicle. Initially I vehemently expressed concerns with the termination, particularly because lessor disciplinary actions were often recommended, by this same director, for much more serious offenses. When I did so I was not only accused of an inappropriate relationship, I was questioned as to whether or not I was able to do my job objectively. Based on my inexperience and fear I yielded to the demand for his termination. That sowed a seed of doubt into my decision-making. My focus was on whether a decision would be supported rather than if my decisions were just.

For a while after, I made decisions designed around others as opposed to what I knew, and believed, were professionally correct. I was not being authentic in these moments. I was afraid, doubtful and not the best representation of a woman in leadership. I did what so many other women who hold these roles do. I succumbed to tactics. We may serve in a position but, ultimately, we can become puppets, repeating cycles of how things have always been. We need to be careful.

I had to do a thorough self-assessment as to why I could not stand firm in that decision-making moment. I was always well-spoken, and outspoken, and stood firm on my beliefs and values. Why was this time so different? It was because the system trained me that keeping my job depended upon my keeping my head down. This reality was a hard pill to swallow. It taught me a valuable lesson about fear. If you are not aware or prepared, others can quickly project their fears onto you. Though I learned over the years that followed to quell the ability of others to burden me with their fears, and experienced great success as a result, I soon learned life is an ever-changing journey to remind us of how we got here.

In leadership two things are certain, change and tests. Just when you've beaten one hurdle like fear, something happens that tests milestones, growth and principles. No matter your preparation, leaders must stand ready to make tough decisions. Even if it means risking what you've worked for coming to an end, and you need to start again, it is a risk worth taking.

From professional awards, recognitions, national board appointments and making history as the city's first female and African American appointed human resources director in fifty years, my twenty-year career was quite impressive. It seemed that I had finally arrived and could enjoy the fruits of all my hard work and sacrifices. Little did I know my greatest test was yet to come.

I am an advocate for women and creating leadership opportunities. You can imagine how honored I felt to work with the city's manager. She was incredibly skilled. With more than thirty years of public sector experience, she was second to none. Her stellar history of excellence with the largest county in the state wasn't enough to shield her from sexist comments, sabotage, harassment and questioning by men and women alike when, after serving for three years without an evaluation or pay review, she requested one. She asked to be compensated equal to her accomplishments and the pay scale of her predecessor. This is something all too often experienced by women in leadership; an unspoken expectation to perform without additional compensation. In fact, the example of a single mother barely making $20,000 a year, while feeding eight children and keeping a roof over their heads, was the justification used by one person when they denied her raise request. It was one of the most disturbing experiences of my career.

When she forcibly resigned, I was suddenly confronted with the decision to remain with an organization that no longer promoted or supported women in leadership, or to leave. I chose to leave my hard-earned six-figure salary, company vehicle, defined benefits pension, contacts and business relationships to begin again in the absence of fear and doubt. It was, for me, a rediscovery of my fearlessness!

Overcoming Fear and Doubt

Do you remember being a kid and playing with your friends in the streets without fear of getting hit by a car? When you said, 'See ya tomorrow', you knew you would. Children see endless possibilities. Their minds are open, free to try just about anything. As experience steals youth that carefree, fearless spirit dissipates. As we experience disappointments we lose a bit of our free spirit, our sense of safety. That lack of stability breeds fear which results in doubt. Rediscovering, and redefining, our free spirits as adults helps us to remove fear from our leadership journey.

Fear can take over anyone, even the most successful and confident. Oprah Winfrey revealed that she was scared before giving her commencement speech to Harvard graduates in 2013. She was intimidated by the prospect of standing up in front of the graduating class and was thrown by the request. Oprah acknowledged:

"It came at a time in my life when I felt vulnerable and every single headline was about Oprah and the struggling network, so I thought, what could I possibly say to them when I'm amid the struggle? But you have more to say during the struggle than you do when you're on top."[24]

Our willingness to be vulnerable, to acknowledge our fears, is an effective and rewarding way to overcome them.

We can also overcome fear by being more self-aware. Honest self-observation and diagnosis are key here. Some of the world's top leaders and influencers have contributed their success to this practice. Remind yourself daily of your accomplishments and the sacrifices you've made to earn them. Feed your doubts with positivity. We all need the reassurance of just how awesome we are so don't hesitate to call anyone who loves and supports you for that boost.

Now here is an unorthodox approach that you may not hear very often. Go ahead and allow yourself to sit in your fear and doubt. When doing so be sure to recall the last time you felt this way and remember what happened. You survived, you lived to reflect and overcome again.

Face Your Fears

There is a popular saying, feel the fear and do it anyway? This is exactly what I mean by allowing yourself to momentarily sit in it. When you face your fears head-on that's acknowledgment. When you can acknowledge you are now prepared to change, there is freedom to act in the absence of fear. Acknowledging fear is a necessary component in preparing for, and in sustaining, leadership.

If you ever want to know what freedom looks like close your eyes and lift your head to the sky. Picture clear blue skies and the warmth of the sun soaking into your skin. Basking in this vision you'll hear birds soaring high and carefree. Can you see the one out front, leading the V-formation through the clouds? They are letting you know they are united and, together, they are accomplishing important feats. It is in the sound of their wings, the song on their beaks. The sight of their synchronicity is magnificent! Be a leader who helps your teams to soar. Are you ready? Open your eyes and remember what freedom sounds like. You can do this! Give yourself permission to be free of fear's limitations and soar!

Since fearlessly starting over I've unexpectedly reconnected with my creativity. This awakening has produced some of the most forward-thinking, out-of-the-box approaches to complex issues and decisions I have ever experienced. Some define creativity as the ability to transcend traditional ideas, rules, patterns or relationships and create meaningful new ideas, methods and interpretations.

I'm reminded of a woman who transcended traditional ideas and patterns, indeed creating a new, meaningful pathway. In May 2018, Stacey Abrams became the first black woman to receive the gubernatorial nomination of a major party in American history. Her nomination was one the State of Georgia had not seen in more than fifteen years. On November 6, 2018, Abrams continued to transcend tradition "outpacing President Barack Obama and Secretary of State Hillary Clinton in voter turnout, tripling the turnout of Latinos and Asian Americans and more than doubling the youth participation rate."[25]

I'd like to think Ms. Abrams, sat in her doubt of beating those significant odds. I'd like to think she thought long and hard about the what ifs, fearful of what her opponent may say about her, true or false. No matter her process to get there, she dared to be fearless and powerful. She designed a creative vision that others could get behind.

Stacy Abrams is one of many examples of brave, out-of-the-box leadership, absent of fear that will continue to be the driving force behind every woman leader that decides to stand in her power. Fear will always exist. It will always be the invisible force. It is also defeatable!

HIGH HEEL REFLECTIONS

❖ Rediscovering and redefining our free spirits as adults helps us to remove fear and doubt from our leadership journey.

❖ Fear is not a spiritual emotion.

❖ In the presence of fear, doubt ensues followed by the derailment of your defined destiny to power and leadership.

❖ If we are not careful, we can repeat cycles of how things have always been.

❖ Acknowledging fear is a necessary component of leadership.

❖ Fear will always exist, but we can defeat the limiting thoughts and break through.

Questions:

✓ Are you able to acknowledge your fear(s)?

_____

_____

_____

✓ How does fear show up in your leadership?

_____

_____

_____

✓ Does fear keep you from considering a new venture or leadership role?

_____

_____

_____

High Heel
Leadership
is Freedom

POWER AND AMBITION

"Thou wouldst be great, Art not without ambition, but without the illness should attend it."Spoken by Lady Macbeth, Act 1, Scene 5 of Macbeth[26]

Power is often synonymous with men who have attained C and E-suite corporate status, wealth and/or celebrity. Men are often groomed for these roles. They are taught to win, and praised for their powerful positions, no matter the costs paid to obtain them. Women have made steady strides towards positions of power, charting ambitious paths, pioneering changes for women in leadership throughout history. From sports to public office, women have courageously shaped world-views, global policies and humanitarian services. Why then is having both power and ambition frowned upon when the person leading the charge wears high heels?

In Jennifer O'Connell's article, Ambition: Why is it still a dirty word for women,[27] she writes,

"For women, ambition is sometimes seen as a dirty word. The rationale seems to go that it's one thing to have success foisted upon you; it is another, entirely less lovely, thing to actively hunger for it. If you're a woman, saying you got lucky is fine. Saying 'I deserve this because I worked so hard to get it' is still, even in a more feminist world, much less socially acceptable."

As Lady Macbeth alludes, there is illness in ambition. Ambition itself is harmless but the things some do in its name can be something else all together. Backstabbing, lying, downplaying a colleague's abilities, not being inclusive, handshaking deals in bad faith, gossiping are just a few ills of ambition. Because femininity is not perceived as embodying many of these behaviors, ambition is still viewed as man's work. In order to rewrite leadership we must rethink ambition. Ambition without connection is an illness of ambition.

Ambition Without Connection

If you are truly an ambitious woman leader you will probably admit that, from time to time, you have had tunnel vision, focusing solely on the elevation of your career. We can all be guilty of this. Too tired to expend any extra energy to key relationships, totally focused on our career goals, we sacrifice some of the people, and things, in life that truly matter.

A young woman moved to a new city with her husband and reached out to me for career advice. She had taken a few years off to care for her newborn. Now that her child was school-aged, she decided to re-enter the workforce. The change turned out to be a little more than she anticipated. When the position came to an end she contemplated a different strategy. She considered moving out of state, away from her young child and husband, to revitalize her career. I thought that was pretty ambitious. When she asked for my thoughts, I immediately reflected on my time as a young parent with little ones, driven by ambition to accomplish my leadership goals. I certainly could, but would not, give my opinion about a decision that should be made between her and her family; however, I did share this.

Sacrifice is inevitable when you decide to actively pursue your goals. Wanting more for my children and myself, my ambition for more, became my primary focus. My children learned independence, determination, drive, achievement and self-sufficiency, both through circumstance and example.

There were a few realities I had to come to terms with too. First, I didn't show them the importance of staying connected to what matters, family. I lost people I thought were good friends along the way. Most importantly, my children didn't get the benefit of a fully-engaged mom. Today, they are adults and we don't talk, or share what's happening in their lives, as often as I would like.

I yearn to just hold them while they tell me about their day, to help them through what they believe are life crises. Instead, I watch them do exactly what I taught them, by my example, to be. They are independent, determined and self-sufficient. I implored her to consider what matters in her life and to balance her ambitions against their affect on those matters.

I encourage every woman to relentlessly go after their leadership ambitions. In the pursuit never forget that ambition without connection is a dangerous thing. It is never too late to have a wake-up call or to re-prioritize. Like anything you neglect though, it may take some time to rebuild, especially those relationships.

Aside from your family, there are three must-connections you should make while pursuing your ambition: a connection with self, with others and with your divine purpose.

Connection to Self

Do you know the rhythm of your heartbeat? How many breaths do you take in sixty seconds? When's the last time you asked yourself if you're okay? The hardest connection to make is with self, but it is by far the most important. Many associate hitting the gym or taking yoga classes as connecting with self.

These are needed for our overall well-being but I'm referring to a deeper connection. I describe it as soul touching or tapping into your consciousness. These connections are guides to recognizing subconscious ailments. It's a self-awareness that extends into your leadership roles and differentiates good leaders from great ones. Until you connect with yourself, how can you truly connect with others? Without self-awareness you cannot place value on the analysis you give to interactions with others because you have no solid measuring tool. Your perception is fluid, colored by emotion and experiences, more than by a solid understanding or foundation.

Connection To Others

Remember the hula hoop? The objective was to sustain the hoop, on any part of your body, so long as it didn't touch the ground. It was awkward at first but after lots of practice, and many failed attempts, you felt amazing when that hoop stayed effortlessly on your waist. You even got fancy with it, navigating the hoop from waist to shoulders, from shoulders to neck and so on. Connecting with people is very much like the hula hoop. It is uncomfortable at first but, with practice, you quickly realize how rewarding those connections can be.

When we establish connections as leaders, we're able to successfully build and sustain high-performance organizations. When we achieve a level of excellence, we must remember that others helped us there. This connection may come in the form of advocacy, like using your platform to support, build up or speak out on behalf of, other women. We can't do this alone. That realization will not only reinforce the importance of connecting with others but aide in building the kind of relationships needed to get, and stay, you in leadership roles.

Connection to Purpose

I started this chapter with a quote from William Shakespeare's Macbeth. Here, Lady Macbeth recognizes the ambitious nature of her husband but is concerned that he doesn't possess what she believes are the necessary ruthless personality traits to become King. Lady Macbeth wanted her husband to attain power by any means necessary, even if that meant deceit and murder. King Macbeth's nature did not lend to his acquisition of power through the ills of ambition.

This quote is synonymous with my philosophies of power and ambition. Both are only good when connected to a purpose above self, and for the greater good of others. Absent connectors, leadership is replaced by dictatorship. There is no need to win at all costs. Creating divisive workplaces, backstabbing, destroying careers to appease others or carrying out destructive orders are the ills of ambition. Leaders realize, power is attained, and sustained, when ambition meets connection followed by the creation of purpose!

As leaders we should earnestly strive to create purpose-driven cultures. Purpose-driven cultures encourage and embrace all employee's unique abilities. A sense of belonging and being a part of something bigger than oneself is experienced in purpose-driven organizations. In 2020, millennials will make up nearly 46% of the workforce[28]. How are you leading, preparing your business through, and for, this talent transition? Competitive benefits packages and clever incentives alone will not yield long-term talent attraction or retention. Committing to an organization depends on an employee's ability to connect to purpose. As a human resources practitioner for more than ten years, someone who studied and analyzed employment retention trends, purpose-driven organizations are the 21st century leadership model.

Power Through Adversity

Going through adversity can test everything you thought about yourself and your abilities. I've certainly had my share of adversities. I got through them. You will too. Knowing how is the foundation of great leadership.

A couple of weeks before my daughter's eighteenth birthday, and a few months shy of her high school graduation, she hurt her knee playing soccer. With torn ligaments, arteries and muscles, she needed two major surgeries and weeks of physical therapy. I watched in amazement, and admiration, as this young lady powered through what could have been a prolonged recovery and overcame her adversity. She not only fully recovered, in record time, she obtained the credits needed to graduate, from home mind you, then walked *in heels* across the stage to receive her high school diploma! One day I asked her how she had gotten through it. She replied, 'I didn't want to stay in that feeling of helplessness. I knew I had to get better, so I chose to push myself.' My daughter reminded me that women simply do. We survive. We push through. We rarely allow adversity to defeat us.

Did you know that you could also acquire power through adversity? I took over as a department lead. Having worked with a lot of the staff in previous positions, I never thought that things would become as contentious as they did. I had no idea what was waiting for me.

Before long, a department investigation was initiated and I was being accused of discrimination and workplace harassment. I knew the allegations were not true. Trying to power through that was challenging. It didn't allow me to focus the way I needed to for our success. I couldn't help but think about what could happen to my reputation, my job and everything I'd worked so hard to build. In those moments, I powered through the adversity by reminding myself of my purpose.

When our abilities are questioned, or someone complains about how we may have handled a matter, we tend to take it personally. Don't! I know that's easier said than done. Taking criticisms personally will create unnecessary challenges and could lead to adversarial relationships. In leadership critiques, accusations and attacks come with the territory. We must make peace with that to succeed. I refer to this collection of distractions as noise. Disconnect from the noise and reconnect with your purpose. When you do, strategize and expect a powerful outcome.

Take a few minutes to think about a challenging workplace situation you were in. What did you learn from it? Were you able to later apply that knowledge or use it as an example for another to learn from? There is power in learning from our tough experiences. They help us design enhanced methods of interacting. The next time an issue has you up in flames don't just feel the fire, address the fuel that ignited it. Design solutions that not only extinguish it, but suffocate the likelihood of it catching again.

Embrace Your Power

There is not one person desirous of it who has attained power without first believing they should have it. The process of becoming powerful starts with thinking and speaking that power into existence. Throughout your career, people will question your leadership ability and block your advancement trajectory. The heat is on when your success causes those less than secure in their abilities to question their shine. Referencing women as menopausal, old, loud, aggressive, hot and nice are all tactics used to undermine the power of women in leadership. Presidential hopeful Hillary Clinton was called a nasty woman by her opponent as an attempt to push her off the road to the White House. Nancy Pelosi was called crazy. I have been labeled as emotional and too attached.

This is why self-proclamation of your power is so important. The overwhelming scrutiny and public opinion will crush you if you fail to believe in, and fully embrace, your power.

From the start of my public sector career, I dressed for the position I wanted and prepared for the ones others said I couldn't have. I found power in beating the odds. I completely embraced it. I have a competitive nature. That made some uncomfortable. Early in my career, I found myself thinking about how my competitive spirit made others feel. I had to learn it is not my responsibility to make anyone comfortable. Acknowledge your truths. Embrace them. Then live them through your position of power.

Grace and Power

We stand on the shoulders of powerful women who, despite the odds, cracked glass ceilings - refined in their stance, approach and movement - so we could break through them. Historically, women have fought. They fought for the right to work, receive equal pay, vote and end gender bias in the workplace, just so they could be heard. When I consider all that women, throughout history, have endured with incredible grace and power, with me in mind, I'm honored. I feel compelled to go further than the women before me were allowed to or could. It is a privilege to follow in their footsteps, an architect of new paths for women to build upon. I want to take a moment to recognize their display of exemplary high heel leadership. Some of today's shining examples include United States senator and 2020 presidential candidate Elizabeth Warren, American sports journalist Jemelle Hill, professional athletes Serena and Venus Williams, gun control activist Emma Gonzalez, founder of the #metoo movement and activist Tarana Burke and plus-size model Ashley Graham.

Oprah Winfrey is a media executive, actress, talk show host, television producer and philanthropist. Her talk show, The Oprah Winfrey Show, - It is a privilage to follow in their footsteps, an architect of new pathsfor women to build upon. – should be an architect a new path for women to build upon.[29] The show was nationally syndicated.

When accused of single-handedly causing a decline in beef sales, and sued by the Texas cattle industry, according to court documents Winfrey said, *"I am a black woman in America. Having gotten here believing in a power greater than myself, I cannot be bought. I answer to the spirit of God that lives in us all."*[30]

Under attack, her poise, grace and powerful self-awareness proved victorious. United States Supreme Court Justice Sonia Sotomayor stood firm in her convictions too. With grace and power she penned a dissenting opinion that would change Ferguson, Missouri's law enforcement search and seizure tactics. She challenged the majority and called out constitutional law application disparities for minorities and low-income individuals.[31]

Theresa May became only the second female prime minister of the United Kingdom and Leader of the Conservative Party in 2016. She recently announced her resignation after increased public scrutiny when plans to have the UK depart from the European Union failed in Parliament. Rather than go low, Prime Minister May went high explaining it was, *"in the best interests of the country for a new prime minister to lead Britain through the Brexit process."*[32] Taking responsibility for the failure, the fearless leader admitted, *"I have done my best. I have done everything I can to convince MPs to back that deal. Sadly, I have not been able to do so."*

A lawyer, academic and university professor of social policy, law and women's studies Anita Hill, became the unsolicited face of a woman who experienced sexual harassment in the workplace. She boldly told the world her truth and gracefully endured scrutiny and judgment for exercising her voice.

Today, Ms. Hill lectures around the country and has become an advocate for women of workplace sexual harassment.

Last, but certainly not least, is a woman many of you will not know. Working for more than 50 years without pay, a virtuous housewife, homemaker, caregiver, teacher and disciplinarian, this woman gave up her dream of becoming a journalist to raise seven children. She devoted her life to a purpose higher than her own and sacrificed beyond measure to do so. My mother, Carolyn Hampton, defined her measure of success and remains my first living example of a woman of grace and power. She, and women of her ilk, are reminders of those unsung powerhouses that gracefully endure. They remain committed to the plight of women, fighting in and out of boardrooms, and the public eye.

HIGH HEEL REFLECTIONS

❖ Ambition is good but, without connection, is dangerous.

❖ While pursuing your ambition always keep in the forefront your connection with others, self and divine purpose.

❖ Consider what matters and balance your ambitions with life.

❖ As leaders we should earnestly strive to create purpose-driven cultures.

❖ In leadership critiques, accusations and attacks come with the territory. It's your choice to listen.

❖ Acknowledge your truths. Embrace them. Live them through your position of power.

Questions:

✓ How has ambition positively and/or negatively influenced your relationships?

_____

_____

_____

✓ Do you shy away from confrontation or controversial decisions? Why/not?

_____

_____

_____

✓ What can you do more of to ensure you're connecting with others, yourself and your purpose?

_____

_____

_____

High Heel
Leadership
is Homage

Same Sex Sabotage -
Our
Dirty Little Secret

For some, our experiences in the workplace are riddled with jealousy. That b*tch thinks she's all that! Do you see what she wore to work today? She's too bossy.

No matter the phrasing, the resulting damage has long-term implications for women in leadership. Women are both the greatest supporters, and critics, of other women. I call same sex sabotage the S Factor.

If you're a woman whose has had these thoughts, or spoken these words, don't beat yourself up about it. Do gain a deeper understanding of yourself. That starts with acknowledging the role you may have played in creating obstacles.

This chapter is intended to spark the dialogue necessary to eradicate the S factor and move us past this dark secret. It is a beautiful goal, though I can't help but wonder, are we really ready?

What happens when another woman won't let you be great? What do you do when a woman sets out to destroy your reputation? How do you respond when a woman attempts to interfere with your career advancement?

I thought I had a promising career in banking. Product sales, like checking and savings accounts, were starting to shape the banking industry and I was dominating the space. I reported record sales each month and played a huge role in getting my branch, and manager, recognized by corporate. In spite of all my accomplishments this was still the absolute worst workplace experience

I've had to date. The workload was hectic. I would tend to customer needs all day, nonstop, but those things were part of the territory. I was servicing customer needs and I loved it.

What made it miserable was my female supervisor. Every day, her eyes filled with detestation, she hated on me. Her countenance screamed I don't want you here! She made my daily work life hell. Her tone was always unpleasant. She never reciprocated courteous gestures, like greetings or thanks. She once said I should wear clothes that were more corporate-appropriate on a day I wore an African-inspired top and skirt. She would constantly interrupt my lunch breaks, questioning how much longer I had as I needed to 'get back to work'. Any time I had a male client at my desk she'd find her way over to chastise or ask questions, insinuating I had incorrectly completed another task. She even went so far as to tell the regional vice president I wanted her job so I needed a tight leash.

Unfortunately, there is no way to avoid toxic people. I've had some of my best, and worst, experiences with other women in the workplace. We can either learn to deflect, soaring above their noise, or we can go low, fighting fire with fire. Before you choose the later consider the consequences. I did just that and, after about eleven months of her nonsense, I resigned.

There are many instances where women have not been welcoming to their female peers and/or subordinates. No one wants to admit they have added to the problem, prohibiting the advancement of other women leaders out of jealousy, using intimidation or, worse, taking a hands-off approach.

A 5'3" firecracker of a woman, with a 6'10" towering personality and a mind sharp as a Ginsu sword, shared with me her S factor experience.

I was disappointed, but not surprised, to learn that her supervisor would make comments in front of others saying she lacked experience and would not likely be considered for promotional opportunities. To make matters worse, she endured verbal abuse from a male colleague. When she tried to seek assistance from her female supervisor, not only was she not supported, she was told her attitude was too abrasive. She was considered a troublemaker. She tried speaking with the female HR director, who was also a friend of her supervisor. She was told to not make trouble and get through her probationary period.

She got through her probationary period and over the next fourteen years she chose to deal with it. She, admittedly, became complacent remaining with the company until she was downsized.

You can't profess to be a woman who supports women while advocating for some and creating obstacles for others. I dare say, that's NOT leadership, that's cronyism.

After temporarily filling in at a position that paid more than her regular position, one woman's female supervisor chose to oblige a male coworker by hiring his younger relative to fill the opening. This woman had been doing the work, without a pay hike, for two years while it remained vacant. To make matters worse, she was asked to train the new hire after being told she lacked the qualifications to fill the position.

Her supervisor appeared to focus in on her, rather than her qualifications. She was asked to pull her hair back in a ponytail whenever she decided to wear it down. When she spoke up for herself she was told she was a difficult employee and that all efforts toward advancement in the department would be blocked. To escape what she felt was a dead end, she applied for a transfer out of her supervisor's division.

I am by no means a victim, but I can admit to encountering my share of less-than-supportive women. Whether intentional or not (I hope it's the latter), I have endured some experiences that would have shamed or broken other women.

From my integrity being called into question, to attempts to make me appear less than competent, my rock-star work status was, is and always will be, a threat to women who have not fully realized the amazing talent embedded within. Katherine Crowley and Kathi Elster, co-authors of Mean Girls at Work: How to Stay Professional When Things Get Personal, address the "...feelings of jealousy, envy and competition. Women often compete more covertly and behind the scenes. Covert competition and indirect aggression are at the heart of mean behavior among women at work."[33]

In a 2016 Forbes.com article,[34] The Dark Side of Female Rivalry in the Workplace and What to Do About It, two contributing factors to toxicity were referenced, (1) psychological factors (insecurity) and (2) the workplace itself.

Building a harmonious relationship with a woman who's insecure may seem an insurmountable feat, especially if she happens to be your boss. You may, however, be able to ease tensions and turn things around with an open heart, an open mind and technique. Here are a few tips that have worked well for me.

1. Talk to her. Opening the door to communication may reveal commonalities that the both of you are able to build upon. This is also an opportunity for you to reiterate your support of the organization's, and her, success.

2. If your supervisor is aiming toxic behavior toward you, ask if she would be willing to mentor you. It's not only flattering to think someone thinks enough of you to ask for your mentorship but it's totally unexpected, especially when the person asking is the very person you may have perceived as a threat.

3. When you've done all you can to create an inviting, team oriented and supportive environment, but the workplace remains unconducive to your growth and development, you should certainly consider exploring companies that align with your desired environment. Remember, you always have choices. Never be afraid to opt for a complete separation from toxicity. You are always the CEO of your leadership journey!

The key takeaway here is to realize that these, or any other suggested solutions, are within your control and power. Leaders learn early to control that which can be controlled. While you may not be able to control someone else's behavior, or how they react to your attempts to bridge gaps, you can control your approach to every situation.

Women aged 16 years and older make up 58.6% of the labor force with 40.6% working in management, professional and related occupations according to the United States Department of Labor 2018 Women in Labor Force report[35]. You are not likely to continue your journey in, or toward, leadership without being managed by a woman.

It's highly probable that, at some point in your career, you'll have a female who is a direct report. As is the case with any person in leadership, this can be a negative experience if someone is not mature enough to handle the role.

I am a confident woman with a desire for every woman to feel confident within. I encourage women to shine. I am also a woman that knows when I walk into a room my God-given light shines bright. But even in that reality, I am also humble enough to appreciate every single woman that is sitting in the room with me. Some lights don't shine as bright as others. Because I'm confident in who I am, I can, and do, appreciate what every single woman brings to the table. Collectively our lights illuminate possibility.

As women in leadership we must recognize the lasting effects of unhealthy competition. In 2019, we continue to hear the first female mayor, CEO or city manager and, less frequently, that she is a woman of color. Let me be clear, competition isn't a bad thing. Competition keeps you focused. It becomes unhealthy when leadership opportunities are scarce. Instead of healthy competition, the workplace becomes the survival of the least desirable of our traits as human beings.

Youth and Experience

It is well documented that age, pay and gender disparities between men and women exist. Rarely, however, is the age war among women in the workplace discussed. In fact, I couldn't find a single article on the subject. It does exist and it is a growing concern. I was able to participate in a panel discussion addressing the millennial and boomer dynamics among women. Everything from wait your turn, to climb the ranks like the rest of us, was advised.

Some millennials replied, No. Not if I have the skills for a leadership position. I sat silently for awhile listening to the exchange, wondering what was the root cause for contention. Was it the energy, fearlessness and rebuke of the status quo boomers disliked? Was it hard for millennials to hear how experience and wisdom, acquired only with time, is very much needed within organizations? I pondered how we, as women, start to bridge the age gaps between us.

I John 2:14 reads, "He calls the young because they're strong, He calls the old because they know the way." This passage gives perspective to how we should view experience and youth. We must learn that a visionary isn't such without the executioner, and to build a structure without a blueprint is simply a big block of cement.

Millennials are the most educated group of women in history. Organizations that are working toward gender diversity and inclusion must understand millennials to make a difference in the corporate landscape. This is not to say experienced leaders are a thing of the past. With experience often comes wisdom that cannot be discovered in youth. This is a needed asset. "Look at all the immensely talented individuals who failed during the bursting of the Internet bubble. Many were young, promising business leaders; unfortunately, many of them failed to listen to their elders." - What Counts More: Youth or Experience? Forbes.com[36]

There is both value and power in women of diverse ages unifying. If we create safe spaces for each other, those ready to pass the baton can do so without feeling forgotten in the race and those ready to take the next leg can, uninhibitedly, blaze new paths. We can learn, build and grow together!

Here are a few hard questions. Are you aiding the problem or offering solutions? Let's take a quick assessment to determine what side you're on.

- ❖ When a woman walks into a room, do you immediately introduce yourself or quickly assess her wardrobe?

- ❖ Do you invite her to join you and your group, or do you eye her shoes and handbag?

- ❖ Have you ever whispered unflattering remarks to a woman or made unrequested observations about another woman?

This is a no-judgment zone. I want this book to create self-awareness and positive feedback.

We must be honest about what we do to one another. If you hesitated or answered yes to any of these questions, you must self-examine to determine your personal S factor.

We can all admit that the S factor is a nasty problem. What do we do to fix it? What do we as leaders, or up-and-coming leaders, do to overcome the expectations placed upon us? The solutions start with you! The fight has evolved and so too must our strategies. I want you to understand the role we can all play to bring about needed changes. I want you to continue the fight for more women in leadership positions.

While significant strides in leadership have certainly been made, women continue to lag behind in business and government top positions.

About 20% of the members in Congress and about a quarter of state legislators are women. "Women made up roughly 5% of Fortune 500 company CEOs in the first quarter of 2017 and about 20% of Fortune 500 board members in 2016. As of March 2018, there are six female governors and five females in executive branch cabinet-level positions".[37]

If we don't campaign for each other while our numbers are small, the divide will only grow between us as our numbers increase.

Know Thyself

Have you fully embraced your truths, insecurities and misconceptions? If after initial contact with a woman you sense sabotage, chances are you haven't checked your behavior. Coming to terms with our own biases, prejudices and reality is the hardest thing to do. Check your energy and the message you're sending. Are you inviting partnership or competition, collaboration or isolation, consensus building or methodical teardown? Creating sisterhoods and networks of powerful women starts with your approach and mindset. It will require constant self-examination and self-criticism. Let's always strive for unity by achieving self-awareness first!

Celebrate Other Women

Yes, this may sound cheesy but think about it this way. It is hard to fight against a person who's cheering you on. You don't have to go out of your way to do anything major but here are a few ideas.

Buy a card and write a warm, heartfelt, appreciation. Let her know she's doing a good job. Let her know she's appreciated and look for ways to assist in her leadership process.

Cheer for other women as much as you cheer for yourself! I like to think of my workplace women as being in a never-ending four-by-four relay with me. We run a smooth, consistent race in unison, cheering one another on until we've all crossed the finish line!

Mentor Other Women

Mentoring is becoming more important than ever. We all have experiences to share that can help encourage and motivate other women to lead. From entrepreneurship to creating opportunities for change, mentoring of other women can have lasting effects. Earlier I spoke of the time I asked to start at $8/hour for an executive position. The person who interviewed me, and would ultimately decide my placement, was a woman. This would have been the ideal opportunity for her to mentor a young, unseasoned, driven woman. She chose not to. Women need each other. Lighting the path for other women through mentoring is a privilege. It is a small sacrifice to help someone who may not otherwise receive assistance.

Compliment Other Women

You can always tell when you're being sized up by another woman. You can sense the energy. Rather than feeding into it, I shift it. The same energy, if refocused, can be used to uplift. Who doesn't love a compliment? I haven't met one woman that didn't appreciate someone complimenting her style, her work or her attitude.

I like to compliment women. Women are beautiful. We have unique value worthy of compliment. Make it a daily habit to shift negative energy and genuinely offer pleasantries to women in your workplace. Let's not be afraid to admire, adore and complement one another. It can only benefit us all.

When Women Join Forces

There is no greater feeling than being a part of something women create collectively. I have experienced it and there aren't enough words in the dictionary to explain the energy and power of that space.

In 2019, reports[38] estimate between 3.5M - 5M women lined up on National Highway 66 for the cause of gender equality, protesting a religious ban that prevented women of menstruating age from entering one of the country's sacred Hindu temples in India. At least four women were escorted, by police, into this once forbidden temple. That happened because women joined forces.

A protester named Rakhee Madhavan said, "Social change doesn't happen in a day. It needs time. But with these small steps, we've made it easier for the next generation to embrace it. In this way, the wall of women marks a new dawn for feminism in India." [39]

HIGH HEEL REFLECTIONS

- ❖ You can't profess to be a woman who supports women while creating obstacles for some.

- ❖ Learn to appreciate every single woman.

- ❖ There is value in women of diverse ages unifying.

- ❖ Learn and build together.

- ❖ If we don't campaign for each other while our numbers are small, there will only be a stronger divide between us as our numbers grow.

- ❖ Learn how to celebrate, mentor and compliment other women.

Questions

✓ If you've experienced S factor behavior how has that affected you?

_____

_____

_____

✓ Are you unable to get past the experience?

_____

_____

_____

✓ Have you led, or participated in, the sabotage of another woman's rise?

_____

_____

_____

✓ If so, have you forgiven yourself?

_____

_____

_____

✓ How have you demonstrated change with respect to helping women?

_____

_____

_____

✓ What can you do to assist women on their journey to leadership?

_____

_____

_____

✓ When was the last time you thanked, acknowledged or encouraged a woman in your organization?

_____

_____

_____

✓ How can a female mentor help you?

_____

_____

_____

✓ Have you identified a woman to approach about being your mentor?

_____

_____

_____

✓ How can you be a mentor for another woman?

_____

_____

_____

✓ When will you start?

_____

_____

_____

High Heel
Leadership
is
Acknowledgement

FIND YOUR TRIBE

I n her book, *A Tribe called Bliss*, Lori Harder stated, "Your tribe is abundant access to wisdom in all things practical, professional, soulful, emotional and spiritual" and "Your tribe will help you move forward even in the face of fear, uncertainty and judgment".[40]

I don't know where I would be today, in my career or life, if I had not found a tribe of women to support, uplift, speak the truth to and love me. The members of your tribe are your confidants, advisors, unlicensed therapists, cheerleaders and from time to time, heavy equipment operators, pulling you off the ledge. Your tribe must consist of women from diverse socioeconomic backgrounds with differing personalities, varied ages, with expansive work and life experience.

Don't expect to build your tribe overnight. Building a solid tribe takes time. Before construction can begin you must be self-aware and prepared to be honest with yourself. This is the very foundation to avoiding what I call the mirror effect.

The mirror effect occurs when your friends think, sound and behave just like you. What happens when you talk to yourself for advice or wisdom? You tell yourself exactly what you want to hear. That's not productive. It will prove detrimental in your leadership pursuit.

Build your tribe with your deficiencies in mind. The women you select should be proficient in the areas you find challenging. Trusting yourself, and the process, are imperative to maximizing the potential of your tribe.

Unlearn all the negative myths that have been thrust upon you. Women can't get along. Women secretly plot against each other. She's jealous. She wants what you have. Don't trust her. Women are catty and petty. Though you may, no doubt, experience instances of these behaviors, you aren't able to come into the fullness of yourself, or your leadership, without a circle of women who understand that we are our sister's keeper and only strong bonds will allow you to effloresce. The purpose of your tribe is to keep your head and heart aligned, to yield balanced decision-making.

When building your tribe, choose women that represent your desired personal and leadership goals. I intentionally started my tribe with women who were, by my standards, successful. They were not my friends initially, merely mentors. It took a long while to build and cultivate my tribe. Diverse in age, race, backgrounds and professions one thing is, common they all have my best interests at the heart of their perspective.

Discover the Family Tribe

You don't always need to look far for tribe members. The women in my family were the first members of my tribe. My aunts were strong, bold, experienced women who first taught me to embrace my femininity. They explained the rules of engagement. Everything from refining my culinary skills, to removing unsightly hair was included in my lessons of womanhood. One such lesson stands out and has stuck with me; no matter how much your feet hurt never, ever, take your heels off in public. My aunt said shoes play an important part in how a girl feels, moves and behaves. She was right! Wearing a great pair of heels to an important board meeting always ends well for me.

Know Thy Tribe

I laugh to myself when I think about the sometimes unnerving and complex makeup of my tribe but every member of your tribe should serve a specific purpose. When I want to take a calculated risk, I call on the business owner. If I'm not sure which direction to take, I call on the elder, and when I just need a cheerleader I call on the advocate.

It's like having an arsenal of weaponry ready for any battle. And, like any battle, you must know which tool to use for success. The soldiers in your tribe should be assigned duties to win the ever-present war you have waged on your leadership journey.

Through trial and error, I've learned why any effective tribe must be diverse in thought and experience. The many and sometimes complex layers that make me a woman of power can have my brain feeling like a hangover. I can't always keep it together on my own and having women with varying perspectives helps me to realign. Remember while seeking counsel that you must also be true to you. Don't allow your tribe's experiences to become your own.

When deciding to work and go to graduate school full time, I was told it may not be possible to successfully do both. When I contemplated moving to a different state I was told, perhaps I shouldn't move away from my kids who, by that time, were young adults. When I wanted to implement new unconventional programs, I was told it wasn't the right time so the programs may not be completely supported. None of this advice was meant to harm or discourage me. What I realized, however, was not to seek counsel from tribe members that may have set ideologies based on their own experiences.

Become Part Of A Tribe

For me, there is no greater reward than becoming a trustworthy confidant to another woman. Not only do you get the privilege of providing guidance you, in turn, find yourself a member of a tribe. If you serve in this role, people rely on you for your judgment. They come to you with problems that need to be solved. That's rewarding in and of itself.

Becoming a trusted advisor is a responsibility. Don't take it lightly, or for granted. Someone thought your knowledge and expertise worth understanding. Welcome the opportunity to engage. Help someone build their tribe by becoming a part of it.

Not All Tribes Are Tribal

We all yearn for someone to confide in, bounce ideas off and share workplace situations with. We hope to get sound advice that stays between us and the people with whom we have chosen to share our confidence. Beware, not everyone has good intentions. Ulterior motives are common. They can be devastating when perpetrated by someone you trust. Take Monica Lewinsky and Linda Tripp.

Tripp's role in the now infamous President Clinton and Lewinsky relationship leaves little to be desired. Lewinsky's one-time co-worker at the Defense Department, precipitated the scandal with what appeared to be a stunning act of personal betrayal. Tripp befriended an unassuming trusting Lewinsky and started secretly recording what Monica thought were private conversations. Those incriminating tapes were ultimately turned over to independent counsel Kenneth W. Starr.

I too have been betrayed by women who plotted to overtake, devour and destroy. Be sure to discern old and trusted members from untested newcomers. Because you're constantly growing, so should your tribe. Confidential information should only be shared with those who have proven to be trustworthy and demonstrative of mutual respect and honesty.

Make the most of your leadership right now and commit to finding, or discovering, your tribe of powerful women. Attend well-vetted empowerment summits. Join online community groups for powerful women. Plan female networking excursions. Consider men when expanding your tribe. Finding your tribe doesn't have to be hard. Just make sure it's meaningful, serving and fulfilling.

HIGH HEEL REFLECTIONS

❖ Find your tribe from diverse socioeconomic backgrounds and personalities, with varied ages, work and life experiences.

❖ Build your tribe with your deficiencies in mind. The people you select should be proficient in the areas you find challenging.

❖ You aren't able to come into the fullness of yourself, or leadership, without surrounding yourself with a circle of support.

❖ Trusted information should only be shared with those who have proven records of mutual respect and honesty.

❖ Make the most of your leadership right now. Commit to finding, or discovering, your tribe.

Questions

✓ How will you start to build your tribe?

_____

_____

_____

✓ If you have a tribe, does it reflect positive, uplifting and supportive women and/or men as described in this chapter?

_____

_____

_____

✓ How important is it to be an invited, trusted, tribal member?

_____

_____

_____

✓ What steps do you need to take to show others you're open to an invitation to join their tribe?

_____

_____

_____

High Heel
Leadership
is Unity

THE RULES
OF
LEADERSHIP

"A leader is best when people barely know he exists when his work is done, his aim fulfilled, they will say: we did it ourselves."

Lao Tzu[41]

H ow often have you heard threats launched to get employees to follow a leader? This has, almost always, the exact opposite effect and results in animosity, resentment and disengagement. There are rules to leadership. People buy into leaders and reject attempts to be forced to follow.

Creating purpose-driven teams while cultivating people are key rules to leadership. In no order, these are the rules I live by. You may find some more relevant than others, depending on the situation.

RULE #1 - Communicate

The best communicators are great listeners who are astute in their observations. Great communicators are skilled at reading a person(s). They sense mood, dynamics, attitudes, values and concerns. Communication allows you to connect and is a key trait of a true leader.

RULE #2 - Take Responsible Risks

Leaders take risks, period. Never concerned with failing or if everyone is in agreement, leaders aren't afraid to take untested risks. Traditionally, women have shied away from risk-taking. Sandra Peterson, CEO of the $10 billion business Bayer Crop Science,[42] said "Most women I know who have been successful in business, it's because they've been willing to take on the risky challenge that other people would say, 'Oh, I'm not sure I want to do that.'"

I attribute my vast knowledge of, and success in, municipal government to the responsible risks I was willing to take. If you look at my career, I've taken on a lot of risky roles. To me, it was, wow, this is a great opportunity. It's allowing me to learn new things and take on a bigger role in a bigger organization.

Your risk-taking should not jeopardize the safety or integrity of you, your organization or your team. Assess the 'what ifs' of possible outcomes but don't play it safe.

RULE #3 - Don't Be Discouraged By Unfavorable Outcomes

Her career as an actress and stand-up comedian was in high gear. Her weekly sitcom was seen by millions, making her a household name. She found success and stardom but felt she'd "lose if everybody knew who I really was." She decided to take a risk and publicly announce her sexuality. While some appreciated, many responded negatively. Her decision to stand in her truth resulted in a canceled show, lost wages, nasty headlines and anger. It took 7 years for her to rebuild and find footing once again. Today, Ellen DeGeneres is the highest paid talk-show host on US TV, a recipient of the Presidential Medal of Honor and a trailblazer that paved the way for others to openly celebrate their sexuality.[43]

Not every project or decision will end with your desired outcome. Imagine how different Ellen's story may have ended had she been discouraged. It's okay to be angry and even disappointed when things don't turn out as planned.

But discouragement can halt your major comeback. Ellen knew she was strong enough to come back and so are you!

RULE #4 - Manage People Not Work

If your focus is on doing the work, why would you need a team? Organizations should hire competent people to manage the work and leaders to manage people. It is imperative that a leader recognize their role is to provide the tools, and resources, their teams need. Ensuring training and development as you foster inclusive environments is the role of a leader.

RULE #5 - Ask For Help

The biggest part of exceptional leadership is knowing, understanding and accepting that you need help. Women seemingly find this difficult. Perhaps it reflects historic expectations to prove we can do it all. We are able to accomplish many things without assistance but we do so at our own peril. We can end up bitter, angry and judgmental. When leaders ask for help, we allow those we lead to do the same. That's powerful and liberating! Asking for help open doors for others to shine. Humility is the greatest expression of leadership.

RULE #6 - Prove To Yourself, Not Others

One thing I've learned is that proving myself is always more about my fears and insecurities than reality. Working in prove-mode didn't help me, or my team, it stunted progress. I didn't learn that right away. That resulted in a lot of sleepless, tear-filled nights, and unnecessary turmoil with team members. I learned to stop proving to others and challenged myself to explore strategies that would awaken creativity in my team.

I was once asked to provide a news reporter with my credentials. It seemed innocuous until I read the article. The reporter didn't print any of the information I had provided. It did nothing to change the tone of the article. In retrospect I recognized it was an attempt to obtain proof that I was not right for a position I already had. It didn't sway the reporter's position and, more likely than not, it made me look desperate or unsure of myself.

Do the work of serving others and your teams. Lead with this intent and the proof will be in the pudding!

RULE #7 - Celebrate Your Wins

I don't recall a time that I ever stopped to celebrate the many successes along my journey to leadership. Once I accomplished a goal, I was on to the next one. In hindsight, I didn't allow myself to fully appreciate what I was able to accomplish in my career.

Starting from entry-level to running an entire city as second in command, is truly noteworthy. I've been nationally recognized for my innovative approaches to local government and workplace solutions. I've done so much throughout my career that, by not celebrating every moment, I missed reconnecting with everything that has gotten me to this point.

When you don't celebrate your wins it can feel like you haven't accomplished much by outside standards. Cheer for yourself. Learn to enjoy every moment of your climb to leadership. Toast and celebrate!

RULE #8 - Be Imperfect

Maybe Karyn White was onto something when she passionately sang, I'm not your Superwoman [44]. I didn't get it back then. I proudly, and exhaustively, strutted around with a self-stitched S on my chest. You're not perfect and it's okay not to have it together every second of the day. Life is hard enough without adding pressure. There is value in being an imperfect leader. When something is perfect, growth ends, development is non-existent, and it simply exists. Being imperfect gives you and those you lead opportunity to build, grow, learn, share and achieve together. You're able to forward lead meaning your teams get to lead along with you, collaboratively

Earlier we talked about rewriting the roles of leadership, relearning and rethinking how we see women in leadership. We're not action heroes ready to leap tall buildings in a single bound. Retire your cape and step into your leadership roles. Accept that you'll stumble along the way. That's perfectly okay.

RULE #9 - Build Relationships

Relationships are critically important and will prove necessary in, and throughout, your positions in leadership. Every person of influence has made significant career strides primarily because of the relationships formed and cultivated along the way. Relationships are about how well you and the person you are engaged with can relate. Build relationships for connection and not personal gain. Everyone desires connection and your genuine approach toward relationship building should be mutually beneficial. Your relationships should sustain, bridge gaps and connect dots. Relationships are critical to the success of your leadership.

RULE #10 - Do What No One Else Will Do

Everyone gets excited about doing the work that gets noticed. Instant gratification is like instant oatmeal, done in five minutes. So is your leadership career if your goal is to attain notoriety. When you do the work that no one wants to do, you get to create the blueprint, the foundation. When my company decided to implement an automated timekeeping system most of the staff avoided the tedious assignment. One lone ranger was left doing the work. That lone ranger was me. It was the less than desirable work that would continually propel my career and expand my professional relationships. Do what no one else will take on and the right people will notice.

RULE #11 - Think Outside The Box

We've heard this time and again, but what does it mean to think outside the box? It means take an unconventional approach to problem solving and utilize today's technological advancements without care for general acceptance. It's like taking a simple event and creating an experience. Thinking outside the box is not just about doing it first or right. It's about creating a solid foundation for generations to build upon.

RULE #12 - Celebrate You. Again!

Life will move you in many directions, often without slowing down to make sure you're keeping up. We tend to prepare for the next thing life has in store without taking the time to celebrate the journey we've just completed.

Not celebrating your wins creates resentment and an unhealthy competitive spirit. This is particularly true in the age of social media, where we seem to know in an instant all the great work others are doing. Have you ever scrolled a profile, thought someone was doing more and suddenly felt that what you were doing wasn't enough? Celebrating every accomplishment, no matter how small it seems, is important.

Celebrating you is a great way to remain appreciative. You should remind yourself just how resourceful, skilled and resilient you are. You would do no less for any member of your team.

HIGH HEEL REFLECTIONS

❖ There are rules to leadership. Create purpose-driven teams and organizations while cultivating people.

❖ Communication will allow you to connect, and the ability to connect is a trait of a true leader.

❖ Do the work of serving others and your teams. Lead with this intent and the proof will be in the pudding.

❖ Cheer for yourself. Learn to enjoy your moments as you climb in leadership.

❖ Step into your leadership roles accepting you'll stumble along the way.

Questions

✓ What are some leadership rules under which you govern?

_____

_____

_____

✓ Do you find it challenging to connect with others? If yes, what may be the roadblocks preventing connection?

_____

_____

_____

✓ How do you celebrate your accomplishments?

_____

_____

_____

✓ What constitutes being celebration-worthy?

_____

_____

_____

✓ How do you respond when your desired outcome isn't realized?

_____

_____

_____

High Heel
Leadership
is a Process

VISION ROADMAP

"Vision without action is a daydream. Action without vision is a nightmare."[44] Japanese Proverb

We generally assume people know what a vision is and how it's developed. Terms such as mission, vision and values are often used interchangeably creating meaningless objectives that don't achieve the desired outcome.

To have vision is to have an awareness of yourself, where you currently are and where you want to be, with a clear understanding of how to get there. I'll admit to not having a vision when starting my career. I needed a job! My reality as a single mom of three on public assistance offered little room for visions. I had responsibilities and needed employment. Daydreaming was my norm, thinking only of getting through the day with an occasional, *what if* aimlessly self-discussed. Not until I changed my environment, surrounding myself with dynamic, accomplished people, did I understand that I was not living out my purpose, that my current state was simply not good enough by my standards.

At the start of my career, I saw vision and action at work through servant leadership and recognized how that leadership style changed daily lives for the better. I was inspired and quickly realized that serving others is my passion. This self-assessment, situation analysis, truth and discovery were the building blocks for my vision. I could see the path to getting out of the sunken place, following it to my vision of purposeful leadership.

Follow the Yellow Brick Roadmap

Vision boards are all the rave. Women throwing vision board parties to share their ideal future is a great way to visualize dreams. To avoid playing a grown girl's version of Barbie's dreamhouse though, only a clear roadmap that leads to action will pave the way back from Oz.

Imagine your dream home equipped with an infinity pool, a master bedroom fit for a queen, east and west wings, guest houses, fitness studio, four-car garage and anything else you desire. You can visualize every detail down to the brick pavers that will adorn your driveway. How will your house come to life back in the real world?

How do you go about completing this acquisition? Do you purchase land and build, or do you purchase a home and add on? Do you save over some period of time or do you take a bank loan? Do you make this investment before or after retirement?

The life you desire for yourself also known as your vision is the necessary blueprint to keep you focused on your goals but you'll need a well thought out roadmap to start the journey. Your blueprint is true north on the compass, it directs you toward achieving your goals. It will keep you moving toward leadership success.

Creating Your Roadmap

Dorothy desperately wanted to get back to Aunt Em and her warm bed in Kansas. She could hear the voices of the family she missed and longed to see again. But how? She had a vision but questioned what was needed to get home. After sharing her vision, Dorothy was told to follow the yellow brick road, watch out for Evelina, the wicked witch of the west, and continue on the path until she reached the Land of Oz where she'd meet the Wizard who would help her get back home. These directions would become Dorothy's roadmap to her homeward bound vision.

To achieve any vision you have for yourself, you'll need a plan to guide your direction. Your plan outline strategies, steps toward realizing your vision. This is also known as a roadmap. A roadmap brings your vision to life in a very tangible way. It's the plan that will help you stay the course and keep you focused.

To create your roadmap, start with discussing your vision with a mentor or a member of your tribe. Voicing your vision will get you excited and eager to act toward setting the course. This may also give you an opportunity to flush out your vision and get your strategy development off to a good start.

Your roadmap creation should contemplate risks but not stop you from moving forward. Determine if funding is required to manifest your vision and begin to identify appropriate revenue sources. What additional resources will you need? How much time will be required to put your plan in motion?

Now that you have outlined the roadmap to your vision, are you able to commit all that is needed to reach your destination? This assessment is imperative to separate your dreams from your vision. It most certainly is okay to dream, dream big and in color even. But visions require action and commitment. Your roadmap should also remain fluid, able to be adjusted for alternative strategies as needed so that you're motivated to stay the course.

Why You Need A Vision

If you're anything like me, your mind is constantly working, thinking about the next best thing. Without focus and inspiration those ideas will get lost. Having a vision is the most powerful means of keeping you on task and engaged. A vision will open your mind to many possibilities, unleashing a brighter future. Remember the story of the bank manager who made work not so pleasant for me? Unbeknownst to me at that time, this experience was actually the start of my visioning.

Throughout her chaos and my stress, I would envision managing people, women, differently. I didn't want anyone to regret an employment decision because of mistreatment, my mistreatment. I would often think about how I wanted to make those I managed feel. I wanted to be the kind of manager that would make employees excited about coming to work. This vision was born out of an experience that I didn't wish for anyone. It was born out of empathy for others.

Being the first African American and female chief marketing officer (CMO) was an opportunity to set the bar. I believed in the organization, staff and community. This was an opportunity to showcase and build a brand. I had visions of creating magazine-worthy content and best-in-class programming. I was excited and couldn't wait to get started.

This vision was born out of a passion to set the standard as the City's first CMO. Visions often occur from an experience that leave you yearning for change or improved conditions. When you can envision a future that is better, happier and more productive for yourself and others, you are more likely to make the changes that are necessary to achieve that vision.

I knew the vision I had: to take a nontraditional municipal program and develop award-winning marketing and communication strategies that would be the model for other localities. I realized I needed to know, or help to develop, the vision my team had for themselves and the program's overall results, if we were going to be successful. I earnestly listened; met as often as needed; and took responsibility, and accountability, for their visions. Our goals aligned so when I asked that they trust me to guide their vision and dare to dream big, they did. Together we saw our visions realized.

Here is when cutting and pasting to a board all that you desire, works; even if it is a barbie dreamhouse.

Creating A Vision For Yourself

As a young child, I would pretend to be characters I saw on TV. I role-played with my siblings, even filming a home movie remake of *The Blood of Dracula*. A few years later, I was hand-selected to join my middle school's actors' guild. Always seeing myself in front of others and speaking to large audiences, I would go on to win the first pageant I ever entered and speak around the world about my professional accomplishments. What we unknowingly envision for ourselves indeed manifests itself. Imagine what can happen when we purposely create a vision.

"Vision is your why. Vision provides direction. It's your desired future. Your vision includes what you believe in - your core values - and what you want in your future, who you want to be. It's the powerful reason why you want to do something, your overarching purpose", explains Natalie Bacon, Huffpost.com Contributor.[46]

Creating A Vision For Leadership

"To dream the impossible dream. To fight the unbeatable foe. To bear with unbearable sorrow. To run where the brave dare not go."[47]Dream The Impossible Dream

People get behind purposeful visions, not people. Think about a time when you led your team or yourself, through impossible. You believed it could happen and you made it a reality. Did it have purpose? Could you see how what you were doing would make things better, more efficient or perhaps award winning?

Leaders must create a purposeful vision. It's about inventing, innovating, creating, building, improving and transforming. Some scoff when leaders share bold ideas, imaginative goals and seemingly impossible dreams. But ideas, imagination and dreams are the fabric leaders weave together to create the future and change the world.

Tools To Develop Your Vision

Developing your vision starts with understanding your purpose.

- ❖ Why do you lead?

- ❖ Who are you leading?

- ❖ Are you in leadership for change or is it simply a chance for you to advance other aspirations?

Study leaders that influence you when developing your vision. Become a student of a woman in power and leadership. As organizational needs evolve so must a leader's vision. Practice continued learning through leadership. This will help you evolve your vision.

Dream for others as much as you dream for yourself. People love being a part of something, anything. When it's meaningful, and they can see their place in it, you garner the support needed to materialize your vision.

Make it personal. Some of the greatest accomplishments by renowned visionaries derive from personal setbacks or tragedies. Their life circumstances resulted in the development of a vision that gave them purpose, meaning, goals and the power to overcome the obstacle(s).

Have a tough conversation with yourself.

- ❖ Is there anything holding you back?

- ❖ Is leadership really what you want?

- ❖ What, and who, inspires you?

- ❖ Are you able to identify what doesn't motivate you?

❖ What are your fears and why do they exist?

❖ If you weren't in a leadership role, could you still develop a vision for yourself?

Connecting Vision (Blueprint) and Roadmap (Plan)

Now that you have a blueprint, and a roadmap to follow, how do you bridge the two? Connecting your blueprint and roadmap will not happen automatically. To realize the goals outlined in your plan, you must first free yourself of your limitations. According to Richard Corey author of *The Blueprint: Bridging the Gap Between You and Your Vision*,[48] "All things existing in the imagination must correlate directly to something real and possible." Don't just imagine your dream career. Believe that you can manifest your vision. Believe that you have the tools and gifts to work your plan. Believe when no one else does. Believe in you!

Have you ever seen Disney, Apple or FOX networks recruit a chief executive officer? Such companies rarely publicly recruit for their top position because CEO's are most often selected not recruited. Such selections result from connections made and relationships formed.

Making the right connections with the right people, at the right time, could position you for CEO of the next publicly traded company. Learning the art of networking can help you make the right connections. It can position you on the right path to not just creating your roadmap but executing it. The key here is to avoid burnout. Don't attend every event that's considered the place to be. Try to make sense of when, where and how you're networking by being intentional about with whom you wish to connect. Invest in classes, books or events that teach you how to network. This strategy is sure to help you create a sturdy bridge for blueprint and roadmap connection.

Being an active member in professional organizations can also help to create your roadmap and make your blueprint connection. Organizations such as international associations, chamber of commerce, women's leagues, national organizations, and role-specific associations, have helped me to expand my vision and develop my plan for activation. You'll find, as I have, members with a wealth of experience eager to share lessons learned and to help you make the right decisions needed for successful construct and implementation of your roadmap.

Spiritual guidance is another way to actualize your blueprint. I've developed through my leadership career by allowing spiritual discernment to guide me. This was a necessary stop on my personal journey. You may/not use faith to help you to reach your blueprint. Trust that internal voice to guide your roadmap to blueprint connection.

The Power of Connectivity

People willingly follow leaders that are not only connected to their personal blueprint but whose roadmap to their blueprint intersects with their own. Helping others you lead to develop and realize their vision, while simultaneously realizing yours, is a powerful leadership blueprint worthy of design. While leading a new division with staff unfamiliar with marketing an entire city, together we decided to create a blueprint for ourselves and map a road to uncharted territory.

We became an award-winning, nationally recognized, marketing team for social media content and event promotion for campaign strategies. We developed the county's first web-based, tune-in radio broadcast and livestreamed a televised morning talk show airing twice weekly.

Leadership is not a selfish act. You can get everything in life you want when you are willing to help enough people get what they need.

Expand Your Vision

If your vision for leadership includes you, your family and those connected directly to you, I want to challenge you to expand the vision. We often shy away from taking on a vision outside our immediate reach. Visions that expand past our personal responsibility are necessary for personal growth. Set no limits. Open the doors of possibility to those that are coming behind you. I would go even further. Just like visionaries before us paving the way, you have a responsibility to increase your vision until it frightens you, then sit in the fear until it becomes a vision.

HIGH HEEL REFLECTIONS

❖ The roadmap to realizing your vision includes self-assessment, situation analysis, truth and discovery.

❖ Create the way to your vision by first establishing your blueprint – your destination.

❖ Your blueprint leads true north on your compass.

❖ A strong roadmap to your blueprint will open your mind to many possibilities.

❖ Don't shy away from vision expansion. Be open to visions that frighten you.

Questions

✓ Have you identified your blueprint and created a roadmap to arrive there? If not, how will you get started?

_____

_____

_____

✓ How does your roadmap lead to your blueprint?

_____

_____

_____

✓ What's holding you back from realizing your vision?

_____

_____

_____

✓ What steps can you take to free yourself from what's holding you back?

_____

_____

_____

High Heel
Leadership
is Clarity

POSITIVELY SPEAKING

"Death and Life are in the power of the tongue." –Proverbs 18:21

Going through a few storage boxes in search of documents I needed to close a project, I stumbled across my high school yearbook. Smiling as memory flooded back, and relieved to take a break, I took a seat before blowing off the dust and slowly opening this piece of nostalgia. As I flipped through the pages of time, I found myself staring at my high school marching band picture. Playing in the marching band was indeed the highlight of my high school career. I even had dreams of becoming drum major and decided to try-out my senior year. No sooner had I made the decision to try-out, than loud chatter filled the music room with rumors of who had been chosen. Later that day I even stumbled across the announcement board with the names I'd heard listed, as well as two others, and only three spots were initially open.

I immediately started thinking, What's the point in trying out if the members have already been selected? I really didn't think I had a shot, so I practiced but I didn't prepare.

Meanwhile, I watched another hopeful spend hours preparing for his audition. He'd been in the band room with me. He'd heard the same rumors. He decided to go for it all the same. He said, 'Natasha, I'm determined to give this everything I have no matter the outcome.' I said, 'You do know this is a waste of time right?' He answered, 'Maybe it is. I've thought about that, but I'm not paying that any mind.'

The big day arrived. I went in with no expectation of walking out in the top three. My audition was lack luster and certainly resembled my thoughts. After the auditions, the selection was posted. I, and everyone else interested in the outcome, were shocked! The person who was a shoo-in for lead drum major, and whose name was actually placed on the board as such, was on the list but in second place. It was the hopeful, the boy who spent hours practicing his routine, disregarding not only my negative thoughts but his own, the boy who prepared for the day, he was the person selected to be head drum major. I'll never forget the look on his face. It was the look of a person who always believed it could happen, even when no one else did. It was the look of a leader.

I learned two things that day. First, men are no different than women. We all doubt and contemplate adverse options based on information we receive. Second, I chose to allow what I was hearing to alter my thinking and determine my course of action in a way that was not likely to yield a favorable outcome. My bandmate chose to convert the negative into an energy that kept his thinking focused on the result he desired.

This story is not only relevant to a lesson in growing up but it's a scenario that plays out far too often for women. Those that talk themselves out of a position before they even give it a try. I sure have. But why? Why do our male counterparts appear to go for it while women tend to wait?

How Will I Know?

In 1989 Whitney Houston belted lyrics that seemed to be the year's anthem for women. "Ooh, how will I know (don't trust your feelings) how will I know, how will I know?"[49] Ok, so she was talking about a love interest, but these lyrics rang true for reasons other than love for so many women. It's literally how next level career moves are decided. How will I know is the question many of us have asked when considering career advancements.

How we choose to speak to ourselves internally is just as profound, if not more, than someone saying it to you. We can rationalize what others say but that's not so easy when its your internal voice. Your tongue is mighty. We often see ourselves with a bright future but very often talk ourselves into doubt. Instead of questioning your abilities, which is not positive, try asking yourself questions like: what other skills can I learn now to grow? Say to yourself, I was good enough to get to this point and I'm fully equipped to get to the next. Your tongue can be a double-edged sword. The choice is entirely your own. Speak poorly of yourself and the results will be clear. Speak highly of yourself and the same will be true.

I now realize, and want you to understand, the power to accomplish every leadership goal you have is within you. Despite what we may have been taught, or what has been implied by our experiences, mental incarceration does not have to be a life sentence. Had I blocked the noise, stayed focused on the result, trusted myself as my bandmate had, the worst that could have happened was not being selected. But even with a no, you gain new experiences, skills and confidence that is sure to benefit you in the long run.

It's time for you to see what others can. Remember high heel leadership is about self-assessment and awareness aimed to strengthen your resolve. I encourage you to look within, confront and conquer self-doubt, and speak positivity into your life. It is then you'll discover your limitless talent and potential.

Total Preparation – Mind, Body and Spirit

The road to high heel leadership will not be easy. Past problems will only evolve and spawn advanced complexities. You may be hurt by, or disappointed in, those to whom you were loyal. Sometimes the work you produce will be credited to others. To tactfully tackle these, and other uncontrollable forces, you must be prepared mind, body and spirit.

Training your mind, body and spirit prepares you for the many battles you'll encounter and builds the stamina needed to return victorious. In the movie 300, Spartan boys were trained from a very early age that battle was life's pinnacle. Combat training was customary. Hearing daily how powerful Spartans are, was routine. Taken from the warmth of their home and the comfort of their mothers, young boys were released into the winter wilderness to fend for themselves. They returned only when they were able to defeat the deadly and wild wolf beast.

Develop a daily ritual of thinking and speaking self-positivity. Each day for six days, write on a post-it note one positive attribute. It could be anything, from the way you did your hair to how you completed a project. Place this on the mirror you use to get your day started. Read each one out loud every day and remember what you wrote. On the seventh day, recall by memory all the positive attributes written. This exercise will aid in removing doubt and prepare your mind to receive feedback and criticisms constructively.

I'm sure you've heard your body is your temple. It really is. Your body is like a metal case meant to protect vulnerable yet essential parts that sustain your life. When the case is compromised so too are the life sustaining parts. Regular exercise doesn't have to be hard. Use your office breaks to take a stroll or use the stairs after having lunch. Stand at your desk at least once an hour. Park your car a distance from the door or walk after work with a few co-workers. If you have a favorite food that hasn't made its way on the food pyramid, alternate don't eliminate. I love everything fried but I've learned how to alternate when and how often I eat what I love without eliminating it completely.

Meditate, meditate, meditate. I am a firm believer in meditation but the road to my advocacy was difficult. It's not easy to calm yourself long enough to be present in the moment. When I learned how to be still however, I could see things clearly, developing several options to accomplish tasks. To learn how to meditate, I started with YouTube videos and progressed to yoga for meditation. Don't get frustrated if you aren't able to grasp it right away. Try meditating for sixty seconds and progress from there. This too is a process so stick with it.

Preparation for greatness isn't just about acquiring skills. If this were the case, I may have become the school's second female drum major. Had I prepared my mind and spirit as much as I was prepared physically, I more than likely would have been. Today, I prepare mind, body and spirit. I don't entertain doubt and don't subscribe to predetermined outcomes. Your overall well-being shouldn't come second to skills development. Both are equally important as you prepare for boardroom takeover. High heel leadership is more than just wanting to be a leader it's about the preparation.

HIGH HEEL REFLECTIONS:

- ❖ Your tongue can become a double-edged sword.
- ❖ The power to accomplish every leadership goal is within you.
- ❖ Personal wellness preparation is just as important as skills development.

Questions:

✓ What does your mind, body and spirit wellness regimen entail?

_____

_____

_____

✓ How are you preparing to be a well-rounded leader?

_____

_____

_____

✓ Do you find it easier to give positive feedback to others than yourself?

_____

_____

_____

✓ What will you do to start and/or more regularly speak self-positivity?

_____

_____

_____

High Heel
Leadership
is A Way Of Life

EMOTIONAL
INTELLIGENCE (EI)

"It is very important to understand that emotional intelligence is not the opposite of intelligence, it is not the triumph of heart over head - it is the unique intersection of both." –David Caruso[50]

E motional Intelligence (EI) is key to both personal and professional success. Emotional Intelligence is the capacity to be aware of, control and express one's emotions and to handle interpersonal relationships judiciously and empathetically.

The World Economic Forum predicts that 42% of current core skills will be outdated by 2022, and that, 'Emotional Intelligence, leadership and social influence will see an outsized increase in demand.'[51]

There are a couple of reasons why this is important to leadership. People who exhibit emotional intelligence have the less obvious skills that are necessary to get ahead in life; they can manage conflict resolution, read and respond to the needs of others; and keep their own emotions from disrupting their lives.

In the age, and rise, of technology and automation, traditional leadership competencies such as judgment, resilience and charisma have shifted to meet the requirements of a digital age. Bold leadership and an agile mindset are needed to lead the transformation. The emotionally intelligent manager will be able to shift quickly and find it easier to manage this industry change.

How many times have you heard, emotions have no place in the workplace? As leadership practitioners, we must unlearn and discourage this practice. Being emotional is often associated with being female. We must redefine this narrative and rediscover how leaders should apply emotional intelligence. "People ignore innate characteristics such as intelligence, extraversion, and attractiveness, and instead focus on qualities that are completely under people's control such as approachability, humility and positivity", according to Dr. Travis Bradberry, co-author of the book, *Emotional Intelligence 2.0*, and co-founder of TalentSmart. According to Bradberry these qualities describe people who are skilled in emotional intelligence.

Research collected by TalentSmart shows that people who possess these skills aren't just highly likable, they significantly outperform their peers. What's more, according to the 2016 article 11 Habits of Ridiculously Likable People, "Those with high EI average $29,000 more/year than people with low EI.[52]

Emotional Intelligence As A Science

Before I knew EI as a science, I was a practitioner. If you find yourself being led by your senses or there is something you can't quite put your finger on but you can feel imbalance, your EI is likely higher than average. The following looks at scientists Mayer and Salovey's 1997 model of the four branches of emotional intelligence.[53] These branches bring together the fields of emotion and intelligence by viewing emotion as a useful source of information that helps one to make sense of, and navigate, their social environment.

Following each branch description is a scenario to help you assess your EI through situational analysis and application. The follow up questions are for you to think about as you learn and understand your level of emotional intelligence.

Developing your EI takes time. Consider the entire situation, what is spoken and what is not. Reading between the lines and analyzing your options will aid in your development. Try stepping away from your normal response to a place outside your general reach. If you can assess the unspoken, you'll hit EI at its highest peak.

First Branch: Perceiving emotion - The ability to detect and decipher emotions in faces, pictures, voices and cultural artifacts.

During a weekly meeting a new supervisor to the organization met with staff to discuss departmental processes. Prior such meetings had proven challenging. While meeting, a senior level employee chose to stand away from the group with their arms folded. Several minutes into the meeting the supervisor asked the employee to have a seat. The employee responded, 'No, I'm fine.' The supervisor continued. Shortly after, the employee abruptly left the room. When asked why the meeting continued once the employee refused to sit, the supervisor replied, 'Well, you know, the office is small. Employees stand all the time.'

What do you think the emotional state of this employee was? Were they:

A. Upset
B. Anxious
C. Nervous
D. Tired
E. Eager to participate in the discussion

If you're conducting a meeting and a team member has their arms folded, showing little expression and not appearing to agree with what you are saying, do you:

A. Excuse the team member.

B. Stop the meeting and ask if anything is wrong.

C. End the meeting and reconvene later.

D. Ignore and continue meeting.

E. Discuss with the employee your concerns with his/her behavior.

What were you able to detect from this situation? Paying attention to body language would have allowed the supervisor to identify defensiveness and resistance. The employee stood with their arms folded and set themselves apart from the team. If the supervisor had been empathetic when offering a seat and the employee said no, perhaps reconvening later would have been the most appropriate response.

Second Branch: Using emotions to harness and facilitate various cognitive activities such as thinking and problem solving.

For weeks your supervisor thinks out loud about a specific issue. This is something you witness often but this issue appears to evoke a different, more spirited reaction. S/he hasn't requested assistance from anyone. This is an issue that doesn't appear to be self-resolving.

Do you:

A. Continue working and ignore the self-discussions.

B. Ask to hear more about the issue and offer help.

C. Take control, handle it yourself and keep your supervisor abreast.

D. Wait for your supervisor to ask you to handle it.

This branch deals with the emotions of others. Empathy is the skill and practice of reading the emotions of others and responding appropriately. Asking to hear more about the issue and offering to assist is ideal in this scenario. It may also present an opportunity for your supervisor to hear your feedback, appreciate your ability to critically think and give them pause to assess your situation in the company as well.

Third Branch: Understanding emotions by comprehending emotional language and appreciating complicated relationships among emotions.

You are the type of leader that requires at least two weeks' advanced notice to meet your deadlines. Anything less is frustrating and creates backlogs not easily overcome. The pressure has visibly caused a non-verbal shift in your daily interaction. Though you've met with your supervisor to request additional notice, s/he appears frustrated, even bothered by the additional time requested.

Do you:

A. Quit but not before a vicious tongue-lashing.

B. Talk about it and pray for change.

C. Adjust your workload, anticipating last-minute assignments.

D. Ask that those assignments be assigned to someone else.

E. Offer a plan for consideration and discussion.

The application of empathy, as well as negotiating the needs of others with your own is a social skill required for emotional intelligence. This can include finding common ground, managing others in a work environment and being persuasive.

In this scenario, you've tried speaking with your supervisor to persuade your advanced notice position and it's not likely you'd be able to control if, or when, your supervisor would, or could, honor your request. The common ground here would be to adjust your workload expectations to anticipate last minute assignments.

Fourth Branch: Managing emotions with an ability to regulate emotions for ourselves and others.

You had an early start to your workday and an intense project has kept you and a few team members in the office long past normal business hours. Your staff generally doesn't mind working late but one staff member decided to express their frustration and it got everyone else charged up. They decided to enter your office ready to file a grievance. Just before coming in, you received an upsetting personal call.

Do you:

A. Send everyone home with a one-day suspension for insubordination.

B. Shut your door and ask to meet in the morning to discuss their concerns.

C. Share with the team your mindset because of the call you just received and invite them into your office to talk.

D. Ask staff to file the grievance with HR for the record and meet when HR schedules.

E. Promise to not keep the team past certain hours.

As a leader you aren't just managing people, you also must manage their emotions as well as your own. A highly emotional intelligent leader can recognize when emotions are driving a workplace situation and prevent escalation by controlling heightened emotions.

Sharing with your team about the call immediately makes you relatable. This vulnerability opens the door for you as a leader to be empathetic to your team's issues and theirs to yours. Now you're managing all emotions, including your own, and stopping the matter from turning into an unmanageable situation.

Self-management requires being able to keep your emotions in check when they become disruptive. This includes being able to control outbursts, calmly discussing disagreements and avoiding activities that undermine you, like extended self-pity or panic.

I like to think of EI as a third eye that allows you to see potential outcomes, good or bad, before they happen. Leaders who have been able to assess their actions and emotions, relative to the impact on others, are most successful. International search firm Egon Zehnder International analyzed 515 senior executives[54] and discovered that those who were strongest in emotional intelligence were more likely to succeed than those strongest in either IQ or relevant previous experience.

High emotional intelligence allows leaders to develop sound plans with sensitivity to achieving desired outcome. Your first steps as an effective leader are self-assessment and building your EI.

"An emotionally intelligent individual is both highly conscious of his or her own emotional states, even negativity—frustration, sadness, or something more subtle—and able to identify and manage them. These people are also specially tuned into the emotions others experience." Emotional Intelligence - Psychology Today.[55]

Another characteristic of highly emotionally intelligent leaders is self-awareness, which involves knowing and managing your feelings. This includes having an accurate assessment of what you're capable of, when you need help and what your emotional triggers tend to be which Goleman's model[56] refers to as the sake of personal joy, curiosity or the satisfaction of being productive, empathy and social skills.

Identify the areas that you need to enhance and do the work.

Culture and Emotional Intelligence

Cultural sensitivity has become increasingly necessary in the workplace as organizations continue to see more diverse workgroups. It's certainly not uncommon to see differences in gender, age, race, ethnicity, sexual orientation and religion. How well you develop your emotional intelligence will, no doubt, determine how you successfully resolve complex issues that result from these differences. Accepting and understanding these differences is a critical skill for productive interaction. This is also known as intercultural literacy.

According to Jorge Cherbosque, Ph.D., Lee Gardenswartz, Ph.D. and Anita Rowe, Ph.D. intercultural literacy involves the "ability to understand the wide variety of cultural norms while also seeing both the upsides, and downsides, of all of them. The three skills that make up intercultural literacy are:

❖ Understanding the cultural whys behind behavior.

❖ Seeing the benefits and limitations of all norms.

❖ Transcending your perspective (empathy)."[57]

I believe, just like our views on leadership are changing, so should our understanding of emotional intelligence. A few years ago this was a foreign concept. Today there is no way to avoid refining and evolving in this area.

As leaders it is our duty to become more self-aware. Our own issues, prejudices and exposure must build a more granular awareness of our emotions and embed positive behavioral habits through repeat practice. We must also lead others to develop emotional intelligence approaches and provide blended advancement to EI expansion. Once developed, EI can have a significant impact on well-being, leadership, organizations, job performance and engagement.

This is not a one-step development process. It is an attainable skillset that takes practice. Emotional Intelligence is not going away. More and more, employers are recognizing and acknowledging the benefits of emotionally intelligent leaders. High performing organizations and leaders have discovered the benefits of EI, relative to productivity, and the overall well-being of key stakeholders.

HIGH HEEL REFLECTIONS

❖ Emotion is a useful source of information that helps one to make sense of, and navigate, a social environment.

❖ Properly reading between the lines, and analyzing your options, will aid in your development.

❖ Use emotions to harness and facilitate various cognitive activities.

❖ An emotionally intelligent person is highly conscious of his or her own emotional state.

❖ How well you develop your emotional intelligence will determine how successful you become at resolving complex issues.

Questions

✓ How important do you think EI is to your growth and development?

_____

_____

_____

✓ Are you able to determine your level of emotional intelligence?

_____

_____

_____

✓ How can you apply EI to your decision-making and everyday interactions?

_____

_____

_____

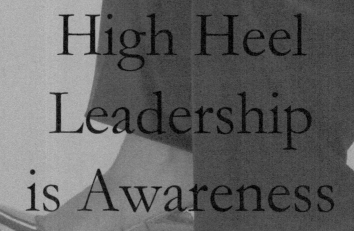

High Heel
Leadership
is Awareness

REINVENTING YOURSELF

"Life isn't about finding yourself. Life is about creating yourself."[58] George Bernard Shaw

Have you ever heard the saying, there is nothing new under the sun? Well this isn't necessarily true. When old habits, attitudes, relationships and structures are re-engineered, redesigned, rebranded or reinvented, we're able to create a new dawn.

Reinvention is the action or process through which something is changed so much that it appears entirely new. Business as we know it is changing and calls for the rise of new leaders. Those leaders will understand how to drive growth, at a substantial rate of returns, in technological and data-driven markets. Will you be able to effectively lead in these new business markets or will the sun set on your leadership career.

Reinventing Through Discovery

From utilities to public works, human resources to marketing, I've learned a lot. Although I enjoyed the increase in salary and responsibility, for a while I wondered if I was hurting myself by not specializing in a particular field. Reinvention is born out of change. With every position, I had to reinvent my approach to management. Frequent change is uncomfortable. As my roles constantly changed so did my behaviors, thinking, studying and learning. Discomfort transformed me each time and I emerged a wiser, more creative leader.

Reinventing Yourself Is Paramount

Like any great product or brand, your reinvention is paramount to evolving your career. First and foremost, accept that what got you where you are today might not keep you there, and it certainly won't be enough to get you to the next level. Marshall Goldsmith, author of *What Got You Here, Won't Get You There*, encourages readers to, "look at behaviors that may be standing between them and their next level of achievement."[59] Success will depend on how well you can retrain your thinking and behaviors.

To Reinvent or Not to Reinvent, That Is the Question?

Have you ever had a negative life experience such as a breakup, lost job or a life-changing event and joined the gym, changed hairstyles or bought a new wardrobe? The things that affect us personally most often jump-start a personal reinvention.

Emotional imbalance is a great indicator that it may be time for reinvention. Recognize that your emotions play a huge part in your discernment and decision-making. If you're bored at work or daydream often, spend an excessive amount of time on social media or can't seem to get back on track with your goals, these may be indicators that reinvention is required.

I knew it was time to reinvent myself when I no longer got excited about my work. The organization's values were changing in a direction contrary to mine. Unhappy and unfulfilled doing what I loved left me confused, searching for answers.

Rather than changing my trajectory, I decided to reinvent myself. I explored more challenging opportunities. I took a risk and discovered what I had forgotten that I possessed, a well-rounded set of skills that make me valuable to other organizations.

It doesn't matter your age or varied work experiences; you can reinvent yourself without losing your authenticity.

Today most people think of George Foreman as the grill guy. Back in the '70s, he was the heavyweight champ who lost his title to Muhammad Ali. In the mid-1980s, Foreman partnered with Russell Hobbs, Inc. to produce the fat-reducing George Foreman grills that have since sold over 100 million units. According to Fortune[60] Foreman was paid $137 million in 1999 to buy out the right to use his name. It's estimated that he has made over $200 million from the endorsement, substantially more than he ever could have earned as a boxer.

It's been almost 30 years since Madonna became a pop star. She remains relevant, even in her 50s, because she has mastered the art of reinventing herself. Every album is a different version of Madonna. Over the years, her music has ranged from R&B to pop, EDM to rock and disco too. Her look has changed dozens of times.

Madonna has succeeded as an actress as well, winning critical acclaim and a Golden Globe for Evita. She's also been a successful record executive, producer and designer. Always keeping her fans guessing what's next has been the secret to Madonna's long, and successful, career.

Social Media and Reinvention

Did you know that you, the professional and the person, are a brand? Building your brand is just as important as the one you help build for your organization or business. The use of social media is arguably the most effective way to increase credibility and establish yourself as a thought leader in your field. Platforms like Instagram have substantially expanded global reach possibilities, helping to instantaneously build powerful personal brands. When you create valuable content on industry topics, and drive thoughtful discussions, recruiters see your passion and recognize that other people respect your authority. The more you contribute to a specific topic, the more you stand out as someone who is insightful or a subject matter expert. You become a resource for others seeking services in your industry.

As quickly as social media can build your brand, it can destroy it too. Before creating your platforms go through the following exercise to ensure infamy escapes you in a world obsessed with fame.

1. Take an inventory of your existing social media accounts.
2. Restrict viewing of your personal accounts.
3. Know what your brand is and how you want it represented on social media.
4. Consult with social media experts to determine the best platform(s) to use based on #3.
5. Establish content to keep your audience engaged and grow your following.

No Need To Reinvent? - The Story of Blockbuster

Remember Blockbuster Video? Their story is a part of business history that confirms the danger of not reinventing. Blockbuster was a video-rental business offering a variety of movies, more than any competitor at the time. Shortly after opening its first store in 1985, Blockbuster expanded to become "one of the world's largest providers of in-home movies and game entertainment." Once valued at $4.8B, and an undeniable dominant force in the rental market, Blockbuster filed for bankruptcy in 2010.[61]

How does a company go from billions to bankrupt? Leaders sometimes think long-ago developed skills are all that's needed to maintain their relationships and customer base. They can't foresee the need to change because they have been successful. Instead they follow the old don't fix what ain't broken adage.

Blockbuster's CEO couldn't see the world changing around him until it was too late. He failed to recognize the need to reinvent their technology, business and distribution models. Before long digital-ready companies like Netflix were taking away their clients. By the time Blockbuster knew what was happening, they were on the wrong side of history. As of 2019, Blockbuster has just one store remaining worldwide.

Reinvention doesn't have to be drastic. Volunteering, getting healthier, joining a civic or social club are ways to reinvent yourself. Take time to reflect on where you are and where you want to be. Ask yourself if you need to push harder, modify or reinvent. When we reinvent ourselves, we take on enhanced ideologies and tap into unknown talents. You can, and are encouraged to, rediscover your powers through reinvention.

HIGH HEEL REFLECTIONS

❖ Reinvention is the action or process through which something is changed so much that it appears to be entirely new.

❖ Reinvention is born out of constant change.

❖ Building your personal brand is just as important as the brand you help build for your organization or business.

❖ Leaders often get comfortable with formerly developed techniques and relationships.

❖ Reinvention is not always necessary. Assess first whether you simply need to modify or if a push is necessary.

Questions

✓ Can you think of a time when reinvention was necessary to your growth in leadership? What were those triggers and how can you help others to recognize them within themselves?

_____

_____

_____

✓ How do you plan to be on the right side of history as a leader?

_____

_____

_____

✓ How will you use social media to build or reinvent your personal and professional brands?

_____

_____

_____

High Heel
Leadership
is Renewal

FORGE AHEAD

"It is courage, courage, courage, that raises the blood of life to crimson splendor. Live bravely and present a brave front to adversity."–Horace, Roman Poet[62]

During an executive team retreat we were asked to pull a card from what seemed like millions. Each person took a turn digging. Some picked from the middle, others from underneath. When my turn came, I picked somewhere between the top and midway. We were asked not to turn them right side up until instructed.

In that moment I flashed back to a time a few months before. I'd abruptly left my employer of 20 years, moved to a new state, started a new job, saw my young adults off to start their lives and learned shortly after that infidelity had found its way into my marriage. I was alone in uncharted territory and, for a moment, lost.

I'm not into psychic readings but I am a believer in the universe and its energy. With all that I was experiencing I yearned for answers. So, when approached by a self-proclaimed clairvoyant woman to pull cards, I randomly pulled four:

Card 1 - Watch Your Thoughts: It's important to only think about what you desire, not what you fear.

Card 2 - A New Dawn: The worst is now behind you, and positive new experiences are on the horizon.

Card 3 - Healing Heart: You're a powerful healer. Keep up the great work!

Card 4 - You're Being Helped: Heaven is working behind the scenes to help you, even if you don't see results yet.

No one knows what tomorrow holds. For some, this may be the most uncomfortable part of leadership. Just when you think everything is under control workplace situations, or life, happen. I couldn't possibly foresee the plot twists in my life but somehow, I found the courage to forge ahead.

No one knows what tomorrow holds. For some, this may be the most uncomfortable part of leadership. Just when you think everything is under control workplace situations, or life, happen. I couldn't possibly foresee the plot twists in my life but somehow, I found the courage to forge ahead.

Courage is the act of moving forward in the dark believing in, and anticipating, a new dawn. Guided by the wisdom of our tribe, we arrive stronger, renewed and prepared to develop others.

A few minutes passed before we received instructions to turn our cards face up and be prepared to answer. The card I pulled read, 'Tell me three words that you feel best describe you.' I'll tell you how I answered shortly.

"You may encounter many defeats, but you must not be defeated. In fact, it may be necessary to encounter the defeats so you can know who you are, what you can rise from, and how you can still come out of it." - Maya Angelou[63]

The card I pulled during that retreat was timely. I was ready for it. I was ready because my leadership journey allowed me to learn from my experiences without concern for what others thought. The words I chose to describe myself were eccentric, bold and believer.

Eccentric because I now chart my own path. Bold, because I know my worth and had found my voice. Believer, because I believe in people and that every woman is special, unique, gifted and destined for greatness when confident in her skin. It took a large part of my leadership journey to arrive here. It doesn't happen overnight; so trust the process, yourself and your growth.

I was invited to Qingdao and Beijing, China to speak as a big data application and governance capacity modernization subject matter expert. What was quite evident is how the application of data, its scientific analysis, and automation, significantly influences how cities, companies, communities and public policies are formed and implemented. Traditionally women were able to enter the workforce primarily because of the administrative needs of organizations. As artificial intelligence (AI) and automation steadily change the face of doing business, leaders need to envision themselves functioning and leading in the e-suite era.

As women in leadership, how we forge ahead will have significant impacts on our ascension from E to C-suite opportunities. The age of automation, artificial intelligence and data technology is now. Organizations worldwide are on the precipice of unprecedented change in service delivery. It will take an incredible display of courage and tenacity to break through this new age of leadership and solidify your place in it.

Leading In, and Through, Technology

According to the 2018 United States Census Bureau,[64] there are approximately 328 million people in America. A little more than 50% are women. 57% of women have an undergraduate degree, 59% a masters, 48% are Juris Doctorates. 47% have medical degrees, 38% MBAs and 49% hold specialized credentials. Yet, women hold only 18% of computer and information sciences and support services undergraduate Science, Technology, Engineering and Mathematics (STEM) degrees.[65]

A 2011 report by McKinsey Global Institute predicted a national shortage of 140K - 190K data scientists and 1.5M data managers by 2018.[66]

Bloomberg reported that the U.S. financial sector saw job postings for people with big data skills increase by nearly 60% in 2018.[67]

Job seekers with experience in AI, machine learning and data science are the industry's most in-demand candidates. Additionally, AI may create more jobs on Wall Street as better technology lowers fees and increases demand.

Despite the demand for technology and data science professionals, the gender gap is clear and, quite frankly, concerning. Only about 30% of data-related roles were held by women in 2019.[68] Leaders must place emphasis on programs that ensure women are prepared to meet this growing demand.

The future of leadership is in the science, analysis and application of big data. Why? Because it is big data analytics that help companies make more informed business decisions, predictions and revenue/loss projections.

Closing the gender gap emphasis in computer science, economics or statistics and mathematics, must be the direction of education institutions.

To ensure women are leading in, and through technology, organizations must encourage and support programs that increase participation in these fields: partner with institutions offering on-site skills training in programming software such as Python and R or Hive and SQL; provide tuition assistance; offer childcare afterhours for on-site training; support equal pay; encourage credentialed training and incentivize women to obtain specialized degrees/certifications in the field.

The most important change to make is for women to dispel the myth that science and technology leadership roles are gender specific. According to the American Association of University Women (AAUW),

"Between 1998 and 2010, more than a half million people from around the world took the gender-science Implicit Association Tests (IAT), and more than 70 percent of test takers more readily associated "male" with science and "female" with arts than the reverse. These findings indicate a strong implicit association of male with science and females with arts and a high level of gender stereotyping at the unconscious level among both women and men of all races and ethnicities."[69]

Stay Informed To Transform

"Anyone who stops learning is old, whether at 20 or 80. Anyone who keeps learning stays young. The greatest thing in life is to keep your mind young."Henry Ford[70]

A learned leader is a transformative leader. In the age of technology, the speed at which information changes is incredible. Staying informed and open to continued development will remain vital for effective leadership. Techniques for skills, like public speaking or regulatory compliance requirements for fiscal or asset management, quickly evolve. Companies like Amazon are prime examples of why you must stay current, and remain willing to develop to meet the needs of your customers, in order to remain competitive.

What are some ways to become informed? Consider downloading apps and using tools like Google Alerts for constant updates and trending world news. Follow organizations or persons of interest on Twitter and join groups on LinkedIn to learn from other thought leaders.

Venture out and acquire knowledge from other areas of interest. Google Suite is an excellent collaboration and productivity application for this purpose. Reinvent yourself. Adopt the techniques of proven models for personal and professional development. Mirror top performers while incorporating your own unique approach.

Trusted Leadership

I've built my brand, career and reputation on integrity and the principle of consistency. I am consistent in my work ethic, drive, decision making, philosophies, stance, actions and policy application.

John Maxwell, founder of John Maxwell Co., author of *Leadershift: 11 Essential Changes Every Leader Must Embrace*, suggests that in order to gain the respect and trust of your peers you must "consistently exhibit character, competence and courage."[71]

During a budget meeting of team leaders, personnel changes that included identifying staff to be promoted at the start of the new fiscal year, were being discussed. There were five candidates, but one person seemed to become the topic of discussion. Some leaders did not think this person should be promoted and verbally expressed their dismay. To make matters worse, the gentleman in question was sitting in the room.

After several minutes of this unsolicited badgering, I could no longer listen to the clearly bias and unwarranted attacks. Without reservation I called for the interrogation to halt and reminded those in attendance that the decision to promote was that of executive leadership and not theirs. I also reminded them that leadership is about support, assistance and guidance, none of which was exhibited by the group.

A few days later, that gentleman paid me a visit. He thanked me for speaking up on his behalf, especially since I didn't know him personally. Since that day he's sought my guidance and mentorship. He says I became his life coach because he knew I could be trusted. 'You are my inspiration,' he shared.

Integrity is a critical component of leadership and should be expected especially when leading others. Unfortunately, it's not always exhibited leaving little room to take a stand, or call out mistreatment and mismanagement. I saw someone unjustly criticized and took the opportunity to take a stand and pay it forward. As someone had done for me, I chose to publicly advocate for him. Some may consider this courageous but I considered it my leadership duty. I became a trusted member of his tribe that day and hopefully sparked his desire to courageously support others in their leadership pursuits.

Give Back and Keep Giving

I have been mentoring at-risk and high school young ladies for years. I'm committed to ensuring young people reach that to which they aspire. I give back to make sure that our young people have examples of leadership. I'm also committed to civic giving through clubs like Rotary, Kiwanis and organizations like the March of Dimes and United Way. My philanthropy supports youth sports, the arts and higher education.

You may not have enough hours in the day to volunteer your time but there are other ways to pay it forward. An estate gift is an excellent way to give back and leave a legacy. Use technology to your mentoring advantage. Video chat, text, hold meetings online. It's up to you to build a relationship that works. Leaders plant seeds and cultivate others to see what they have not been able to discover.

Through it all I want you to laugh more. Don't take yourself too seriously. Always remember it's your job to show those you lead the possibility of something different while reflecting your uniqueness and ingenuity. Get excited about facing the unknown because you have the talent and skill to succeed.

High heel leadership awaits every woman willing, and daring, enough to walk in her own stilettos. So, step high and forge boldly, courageously and powerfully ahead!

Like finding an exclusive pair of my favorite stilettos, my journey to high heel leadership has been hard fought. Inch-by-inch, I squeezed, wrestled, ached and dared to stand on the balls of my feet, balancing on the heels of women who came before me.

I don't just look at a pair of heels as functional footwear with flare. My heels, and resulting clavus, represent my journey to leadership struggles. They serve as a reminder of the seemingly exhaustive climb to the top women all too often experience.

Amid the unspoken pain and temporarily debilitating spasms, are six-inch platforms of security, power, strength and elevation that I get to confidently strut in each day. For these reasons, I'm selective about each pair I acquire, ensuring the voice I've found can be heard through them.

Your path to high heel leadership should be walked in your best heels. As you place them on, one at a time, I want you to reflect on what you have experienced while reading this book. I shared some of my most personal moments, and some of the highlights, of my life and career. While this process has evoked a personal healing, and new level of self-acceptance, I hope that your experience with the book leads to your own metamorphosis.

As we have become sisters in leadership, I want to continue to grow and engage with you in further conversation. I welcome you to contact me at NatashaHampton.com and share your stories. It is my desire to aid in the creation of a movement of women leaders who are strong, confident, fearless, empowered, feminine, poised to redefine narratives and raising the bar for women in leadership. It is my hope this book is one of many ignitors fueling your flame.

What does an ideal world of women in leadership look like? I would have to sum it up by saying diverse, skilled, collaborative, compassionate and readied. My fellow leaders, are you ready to lock arms and create a dynamic, high-performing environment for yourself, those you lead and for those who aspire to be leaders themselves? I believe you are!

Please don't let this be another book that collects dust after reading just taking up space in your life. As I stated when we began, the face and culture of leadership is changing. As you evolve it is my hope, you'll find this book useful as you define your blueprints, create those roadmaps and guide yourself, and your tribe, toward each new vision board of the future. As traditional ideologies of women in leadership are unlearned and rewritten, we must strive to not just read, but author, the change.

HIGH HEEL REFLECTIONS

- ❖ Courage is the act of moving forward in the dark believing in, and anticipating, a new dawn.

- ❖ Dispel the myth that science and tech leadership roles are gender specific.

- ❖ You may encounter many defeats, but you must not be defeated.

Questions:

✓ How are you preparing to meet the data and technology age?

_____

_____

_____

✓ What will you do to ensure your continuous learning?

_____

_____

_____

✓ How will you author change for you and women in leadership?

_____

_____

_____

High Heel
Leadership
is Now!

NOTES

Introduction

1. National Conference of State Legislators, Teen Pregnancy Prevention, October 11, 2018, https://www.ncsl.org/research/health/teen-pregnancy-prevention.aspx

Chapter 1

2. Sheryl Sanderberg, Harvard Business School Commencement Speech, April 2013

3. Christine Exley and Judd Kessler, Why Don't Women Self-Promote As Much As Men?, Harvard Business Review, December 19, 2019, https://hbr.org/2019/12/why-dont-women-self-promote-as-much-as-men

4. City Council Meeting January 26, 2010– City of Miramar, Florida

5. Taylor Swift, "Ours", Speak Now © Big Machine Records, Album, 2011

6. Facebook, June 20, 2019, Rocky Mount Concerned Citizens

7. Carrie Kerpen, "How Women Leaders Are Building Better Places To Work" Forbes.com, April 30, 3019, https://www.forbes.com/sites/carriekerpen/2019/04/30/how-women-leaders-are-building-better-places-to-work/#2a62f7fd56a4

8. 2011 Global Institute, Edie Weiner, President of Weiner, Edrich, Brown, Inc - Melissa J. Anderson, Women and Complexity: Strategic Multitaskers https://theglasshammer.com/2011/06/16/women-and-complexity-strategic-multitaskers/

9. Psychology Today Article: Dona Matthews Ph.D. Empathy: Where Kindness, Compassion, Happiness Begin,Part 1:Empathy is important, but more complex and nuanced than it seems. www.psychologytoday.com/us/blog/going-beyond-intelligence/201910/empathy-where-kindness-compassion-and-happiness-begin%3famp

10. Gallup Survey: Kimberly Fitch and Sangeeta Agrawal, Female Bosses are More Engaging to Male Bosses, Business Journal, https://news.gallup.com/businessjournal/183026/female-bosses-engaging-male-bosses.aspx

Chapter 2

11. Laura Berger, The Rise Of Women In Corporate Boardrooms, Forbes.com, February 13, 2019, https://www.forbes.com/sites/forbescoachescouncil/2019/02/13/the-rise-of-women-in-corporate-boardrooms/

12. History of Women in the U.S. Congress, Center for American Women and Politics, Eagleton Institute of Politics, Rutgers University, January 31, 2020, https://cawp.rutgers.edu/history-women-us-congress

13. Rosalynn Carter Quotes. BrainyQuote.com, BrainyMedia Inc, 2020. https://www.brainyquote.com/quotes/rosalynn_carter_126340, accessed May 1, 2020

14. Sally Helgesen, The Female Advantage: Women's Ways of Leadership, (New York, Currency Doubleday, 1990/2011)

15. International City County Management Association (ICMA) , June 2019 Vol. 101 No.5 Public Management publication, Rediscovering the learning Mind, Why the Professional Development Leads to Success article by Patrick Malone, pg. 11

Chapter 3

16. Sheryl Wilson, *Oprah, Celebrity and Formation of Self*, Palgrave McMillan, New York, 2003

17. Black Women Disproportionately Experience Workplace Sexual Harassment, New NWLC Report Reveals, National Women's Law Center, August 2, 2018. Press Release, https://nwlc.org/press-releases/black-women-disproportionately-experience-workplace-sexual-harassment-new-nwlc-report-reveals/

18. Courtney Connley, The number of women running Fortune 500 companies is at a record high, cnbc.com, May 16, 2019, https://www.cnbc.com/2019/05/16/the-number-of-women-running-fortune-500-companies-is-at-a-record-high.html

19. The People Alchemist, https://www.thepeoplealchemist.com/dont-get-lost-in-the-fast-fashion-crowd-beyourself-always

20. Madeleine Albright, The Diplomat, First woman to become U.S. Secretary of State, Interview. Time, September 2017, https://time.com/collection/firsts/4883068/madeleine-albright-firsts/

21. Jean Chatzky, How to find your voice at work (and use it), according to these female CEOs, Nbcnews.com, April 1, 2018, https://www.nbcnews.com/better/business/who-are-you-how-5-female-ceos-found-their-voice-ncna895901

Chapter 4

22. Saida Agostini, When I Dare To Be Powerful, YWCA, April 25, 2019, https://www.ywca.org/blog/2019/04/25/when-i-dare-to-be-powerful

23. Night Crawler, Dir. Dan Gilroy. Perf Jake Gyllenhall, Rene Russo, Riz Ahmed, Bold Films, 2014.

24. Oprah Talks Overcoming Fear and Finding Her Calling In the Path Made Clear, Her New Book, The O Magazine, by Emma Didbin, April 10, 2019, https://www.oprahmag.com/entertainment/books/a27099094/oprah-cbs-this-morning-new-book/

25. Stacey Abrams, *Lead from the Outside: How to Build Your Future and Make Real Change*, New York, New York, Picador; (2018/ 2019), page 5-6

Chapter 5

26. Williams Shakespeare, The Tragedy of Macbeth, Act I Scene V, Published 1607, England

27. Jennifer O'Connell, Ambition: Why is it still a dirty word for women?, The Irish Times, October 20, 2018, https://www.irishtimes.com/life-and-style/people/ambition-why-is-it-still-a-dirty-word-for-women-1.3665720

28. Millennials are the largest generation in the U.S. labor force, April 11, 2018 by Richard Fry, Pew Research Center, https://www.pewresearch.org/fact-tank/2018/04/11/millennials-largest-generation-us-labor-force/

29. Oprah Winfrey's Official Biography, May 17, 2011, Oprah.com. https://www.oprah.com/pressroom/oprah-winfreys-official-biography/2

30. Aman Batheja, The Time Oprah Winfrey Beefed with the Texas Cattle Industry, The Texas Tribune, January 10, 2018, https://www.texastribune.org/2018/01/10/time-oprah-winfrey-beefed-texas-cattle-industry/

31. Joseph P. Williams, Sotomayor's Blistering Dissent Rails Against 'Unlawful Police Stops', The Supreme Court justice got personal in her argument opposing the majority opinion on a Fourth Amendment case, June 20, 2016, AAUW, https://www.usnews.com/news/articles/2016-06-20/sotomayors-blistering-dissent-rails-against-unlawful-police-stops

32. Rob Picheta, Theresa May to resign as UK Prime Minister, CNN, May 25, 2019, Chapter 6

Chapter 6

33. Katherine Crowley and Kathi Elster, *Mean Girls at Work: How to Stay Professional When Things Get Personal*, McGraw-Hill Education; 1 edition (October 30, 2012)

34. Bonnie Marcus, The Dark Side Of Female Rivalry In The Workplace And What To Do About It, Forbes, January 13, 2016; https://www.forbes.com/sites/bonniemarcus/2016/01/13/the-dark-side-of-female-rivalry-in-the-workplace-and-what-to-do-about-it/#7e2213a15255

35. Women in the Labor Force in 2010, US Department of Labor, Women's Bureau https://www.dol.gov/wb/factsheets/qf-laborforce-10.htm

36. Aileron, What Counts More: Youth or Experience? Forbes.com, November 29, 2012, https://www.forbes.com/sites/aileron/2012/11/29/what-counts-more-youth-or-experience/#21eb3ccc3bb8

37. Women have made inroads March 15, 2018, For Women's History Month, a look at gender gains – and gaps – in the U.S., by A.W. Geiger and Kim Parker, https://www.pewresearch.org/fact-tank/2018/03/15/for-womens-history-month-a-look-at-gender-gains-and-gaps-in-the-u-s/

38. Kamala Thiagarajan, Millions Of Women In India Join Hands To Form A 385-Mile Wall Of Protest, NPR, January 4, 2019, https://www.npr.org/sections/goatsandsoda/2019/01/04/681988452/millions-of-women-in-india-join-hands-to-form-a-385-mile-wall-of-protest

39. Rosalind Jones, Feminists in India Built a "Women's Wall" to Fight Patriarchy, Ms. Magazine, January 10, 2019, https://msmagazine.com/2019/01/10/feminists-india-built-womens-wall-fight-patriarchy/

Chapter 7

40. Tiffany Skirrow, Why Building A Tribe As An Entrepreneur Is Key To Your Success, Boss Babe, October 18, 2018, https://bossbabe.com/why-building-a-tribe-as-an-entrepreneur-is-key-to-your-success/

Chapter 8

41. Lao Tzu Quotes. BrainyQuote.com, BrainyMedia Inc, 2020. https://www.brainyquote.com/quotes/lao_tzu_121709, accessed May 1, 2020

42. Sasha Galbraith, Bayer CropScience's Sandra Peterson: Successful Woman CEO Navigates in a Man's World, Forbes.com, December 7, 2011, https://www.forbes.com/sites/sashagalbraith/2011/12/07/bayer-

cropsciences-sandra-peterson-successful-woman-ceo-navigates-in-a-mans-world/#5d00ea2435e54

43. Marie Claire, Ellen DeGeneres hasn't had an easy ride in becoming one of Hollywood's first openly gay women, October 10, 2019, https://www.marieclaire.co.uk/entertainment/people/ellen-degeneres-life-story-462038

44. Artist Karyn White, Superwoman, written by L.A. Reid, Babyface & Daryl Simmons, Language of Love Album © Warner Bros., January 2, 1989, produced by L.A. Reid, Babyface & Daryl Simmons

Chapter 9

45. Quotes by "Japanese Proverb", https://tinybuddha.com/wisdom-author/japanese-proverb/

46. Natalie Bacon, Huffpost Contributor, Why You Need to Create Visions (Not Just Goals), https://www.huffpost.com/entry/why-you-need-to-create-visions-not-just-goals_b_6129276

47. The Impossible Dream written by Joe Davion and Mitchell Leigh. Rights held by The Bicyle Music Group and Helena Music Company.

48. Richard Corey, The Blueprint-Bridging the Gap Between You and Your Vision, pg.4, Tate Publishing & Enterprises, LLC, 2013

Chapter 10

49. Artist Whitney Houston, How Will I Know written by George Robert Merrill / Narada Michael Walden / Shannon Rubicam, How Will I Know lyrics © Warner Chappell Music, Inc, Universal Music Publishing Group, Royalty Network

Chapter 11

50. David Caruso, Ph.D. – Yale Center for Emotional Intelligence- quote?, Emotional Intelligence for Success & High Performance: Key Competencies for Success and High Performance, by Granville Ed D'Souza DBA, www.partidgepublilshing.com/singapore, Chapter 1, pg 13

51. World Economic Forum, The Future of Jobs Report 2018, pg. 15, Centre for the New Economy and Society, Contributors- Till Alexander Leopold, Vesselina Ratcheva, Saadia Zahidi

52. Dr. Travis Bradberry, 11 Habits of Ridiculously Likeable People, TalentSmart.com, 2016, https://www.talentsmart.com/articles/11-Habits-of-Ridiculously-Likeable-People-2147446666-p-1.html

53. Peter Salovey and Daisy Grewal, The Science of Emotional Intelligence, Association of Psychological Science Current Directions in Psychological Science, Vol. 14, No.6 (Dec., 2005), pp.281-285

54. Emotional Intelligence as an Organizational Asset by Louise Altman and George Altman, 95th ISM Annual International Supply Management Conference, April 2010, https://www.instituteforsupplymanagement.org/files/Pubs/Proceedings/2010ProcZD-Altman.pdf

55. Emotional Intelligence, Psychology Today, https://www.psychologytoday.com/us/basics/emotional-intelligence

56. Goleman's model, How to Be Emotionally Intelligent – By Daniel Goleman April 7, 2015, The New York Times https://www.nytimes.com/2015/04/12/education/edlife/how-to-be-emotionally-intelligent.html?_r=3.

57. Jorge Cherbosque, Ph.D., Lee Gardenswartz, Ph.D., Anita Rowe, Ph.D., Emotional Intelligence and Diversity: A Transformational Process for Professional Success and Personal Effectiveness, pg.3-4 , Emotional Intelligence and Diversity Institute, scholarly articles

Chapter 12

58. George Bernard Shaw Quotes, BrainyQuote.com. Retrieved May 1, 2020, from BrainyQuote.com Web site: https://www.brainyquote.com/quotes/george_bernard_shaw_10954 2

59. Marshall Goldsmith with Mark Reiter, What Got You Here, Won't Get You There by, How Successful People Become Even More Successful, Hachette Books; Revised ed. edition (February 22, 2007) pg. 95

60. Daniel Roberts, George Foreman: Still knocking 'em out, Forbes.com, March 6, 2015, https://fortune.com/2015/03/06/george-foreman/

61. History.com Editors, First Blockbuster store opens, History.com, Updated: October 16, 2019 Original: November 13, 2009, https://www.history.com/this-day-in-history/first-blockbuster-store-opens

Chapter 13

62. 38 Quotes about Bravery and Leadership, Leadership Inspiration by Conant Leadership, https://conantleadership.com/38-quotes-about-bravery-and-leadership/

63. Marianne Schnall, An Interview With Maya Angelou, Psychology Today, February 17, 2009, https://www.psychologytoday.com/us/blog/the-guest-room/200902/interview-maya-angelou4

64. United States Census Bureau, https://www.census.gov/quickfacts/fact/table/US/PST045219 and https://www.census.gov/quickfacts/fact/table/US/PST045218#PST045218

65. Catalyst, *Quick Take: Women in Science, Technology, Engineering, and Mathematics (STEM)* (June 14, 2019).

66. Big data: The next frontier for innovation, competition, and productivity May 2011 | Report, By James Manyika, Michael Chui, Brad Brown, Jacques Bughin, Richard Dobbs, Charles Roxburgh, and Angela Hung Byers, McKinsey Digital, https://www.mckinsey.com/business-functions/mckinsey-digital/our-insights/big-data-the-next-frontier-for-innovation

67. Rodrigo Orihuela and Dina Bass, Help Wanted: Black Belts in Data, Bloomberg Businessweek, June 4, 2015, https://www.bloomberg.com/news/articles/2015-06-04/help-wanted-black-belts-in-data

68. Sabrina Baez, The Gender Gap in Data Science (and What You Can Do About It), Data Quest https://www.dataquest.io/blog/women-data-science-gender-gap/

69. The STEM Gap: Women and Girls in Science, Technology, Engineering and Math, American Association of University Women (AAUW), https://www.aauw.org/research/why-so-few/

70. Henry Ford Quotes. BrainyQuote.com, BrainyMedia Inc, 2020. https://www.brainyquote.com/quotes/henry_ford_103927, accessed May 1, 2020

71. John Maxwell, *Leadershift: 11 Essential Changes Every Leader Must Embrace*, HarperCollins Leadership; 1 edition (February 5, 2019)

DEDICATION

Everything I am is because of Her and everything I am destined to be is because of Him. I dedicate this book to my parents, Cary Hampton, Sr. who passed away twelve months before I completed this project and Carolyn L. Hampton. My gratitude extends beyond mere words.

To my children, Evell Hampton, Saria Blain and Yasharwan Blain, you represent the absolute best of me!

I also dedicate this book to my late Grandmothers Hazel V. Pierre and Sennie Smith, my late Grandfather Charlie Smith and Uncle Darren Hampton.

ACKNOWLEDGEMENTS

To the Most High GOD be the glory, in the name of my Lord and Savior Jesus Christ, I give praise and acknowledge I am nothing without HIM!

Daddy and Mommy, you are excellence personified; thank you. To my brothers Bertron, Cary, Jr., Shenavian (Bean) and sisters Eboni, Autoya and Tehsheka (Winky), I love you. I am forever grateful to the women in my life, Aunt (s) Brenda (Marjorie), Bernietha, Leona, Darletha, Theresa & Kim, my cousins (too many to name) and friends, that have encouraged, supported, lifted, hugged, loved, connected and mentored me. To my sister, Tehsheka Hampton, thank you for big sistering for such a time as this. Thanks to Ellen Woods, Rodney Smith, Michelle Swaby-Smith and Daniell "Danni" Washington, for bringing me out of the darkness right before I started this project. Thank you, Kathleen Woods-Richardson, for the example of workplace grace and strength that provided me with writing inspiration. Lyoness and Carolyn Williams, you both are living examples of God's work on earth. Angie Nicolas, you made all the difference when I needed it most and, for that, I am eternally grateful to you; thank you. Thank you sincerely Bob, for fearlessly making that unpopular appointment. To the person that inspired me without saying a word, CJMB, thank you! There are a number of women and men I'd like to thank; I wish I could name each and every one of you. Your mentorship and guidance have truly made this book possible. To Eulaine Johnson, Dr. Wilhelmena Mack, Dr. Olivia Jackson, Linda Winker, Helen Gage and Sharon Grant, thank you from the bottom of my heart.

ABOUT THE AUTHOR

N atasha Hampton is the new dynamic voice in the arena of thought leadership and women's empowerment. An award winning public administrator, affectionately known as Ms. Red Bottoms, Natasha was raised in Miami's Liberty City, a primarily African American inner city neighborhood where expectations for success was low.

She started her municipal career in an entry level clerical position that sparked her desire to become a female leader in the field of Public Administration. She did the work and skillfully climbed her way to achieve such positions as Acting City Manager, Assistant City Manager, Chief Marketing Officer and Director of Human Resource in Florida and North Carolina.

Natasha was named one of South Florida's 50 Most Powerful and Influential Leaders, and has been recognized as a March of Dimes Woman of Distinction. She has been seen on CBS, NBC, ABC, FOX and PBS and featured in Sun-Sentinel and The Herald.

Natasha is the proud Mom of three and currently resides in North Carolina.

Notable Achievements:

- First live web radio, live stream and television broadcast of a municipal studio talk show in City and County.
- Executive Mentorship Program for students with behavioral and learning disabilities.
- Women's and Men's Empowerment Recognition Program.
- Established Girls of Today Women of Tomorrow mentoring program.
- Developed City of Miramar, Florida's first customer call center and training programs.

Education:

Master of Public Administration, Nova Southeastern University -Huizenga College of Business

Bachelor of Science, Political Science and Public Administration, Florida Memorial University (HBCU)

For Bookings and more information visit:
http://www.natashahampton.com/

Stay connected on social media: Facebook, Instagram, Linked In, Twitter @ highheelleadership

Milton Keynes UK
Ingram Content Group UK Ltd.
UKHW021559220324
439975UK00010B/259